Vienna
A Guide to its Music and Musicians

Franz Endler

Vienna
A Guide to its
Music and Musicians

Translated by Dr. Leo Jecny
Foreword by Leonard Bernstein

Reinhard G. Pauly, General Editor

AMADEUS PRESS
Portland, Oregon

© Österreichischer Bundesverlag Gesellschaft m.b.H., Wien 1985,
as *Musik in Wien, Musik aus Wien*

Translation © 1989 by Amadeus Press (an imprint of Timber Press, Inc.)
ISBN 0-931340-16-0
Printed in Hong Kong

Amadeus Press
9999 S.W. Wilshire
Portland, Oregon 97225

Library of Congress Cataloging-in-Publication Data

Endler, Franz, 1937-
  [Musik in Wien, Musik aus Wien. English]
  Vienna : a guide to its music and musicians / Franz Endler ;
translated by Leo Jecny ; foreword by Leonard Bernstein ; Reinhard
G. Pauly, general editor.
    p.   cm.
  Translation of: Musik in Wien, Musik aus Wien.
  Includes index.
  ISBN 0-931340-16-0
  1. Music--Austria--Vienna--History and criticism. 2. Vienna
(Austria)--Description.   I. Pauly, Reinhard G.   II. Title.
ML246.8.V6E5513 1989
780'.9436'13--dc19   88-7426
                                                          CIP
                                                          MN

Contents

Foreword

Franz Endler belongs to a
vanishing breed: namely, the music —
critic who actually loves music, does
not feel himself to be a failed
musician, knows whereof he speaks,
and speaks it in a prose that's
wonderfully old-fashioned and
yet fresh. How we need him!

LB

Preface

The Viennese say without giving much thought to it: Vienna is a City of Music. Visitors to Vienna either believe this before they have set foot in the city or, once they have been a few days in Vienna, become convinced of it.

Well, is Vienna really a City of Music, and what are the signals and how do we recognize them once we have decided to get away from the phrases always used in tourists' folders?

The answer as I understand it can be found in the following pages. To do so I must, of course, at the same time provide a short guide through the history of this City of Music. And lastly I have tried to offer an aid for those who want to visit or learn something about some of Vienna's places of musical interest.

Basically, however, the reader will find the same answer I did while writing this little book: Vienna is a city in which music is considered exciting—an unusual gift from God, and as natural as air without which we cannot exist. Therefore, music is discussed and written about either too much and in too poetic or scientific terms, or it is simply taken for granted. This latter happens sometimes above all in circles of Viennese musicians who almost from birth are used to, breathe and make music; to them it is strange to talk about it or think about it. For the reader I have only one word of advice: Acquaint yourself with the contents quickly if you are already a visitor to the city and want to learn some basic facts about Mozart or Johann Strauss, but understand that only a few elementary facts can be offered here, no in-depth information. In the end, the reader will realize that it was not Mozart, not Schubert, not only the Strauss family who have made Vienna the City of Music, but that it is the city itself that attracted all these musicians, fascinated them and never let them go. This is how it became, and, we hope, will remain a City of Music for future generations.

I know that there have been many other important, maybe even more significant manifestations of the human spirit in this City of Music. But none of these can look back over so many centuries of distinction and success as does music in Vienna. This, for me— my question and answer—is an important and indisputable fact.

The Court Chapel

No fear of history, please—we have to deal with it, too, but it is not a question of mentioning a few impressive dates. Only: In order to understand how much music was "at home" in Vienna, we have to know how far the line goes back without interruptions.

We do not have to go back too far—only to the 15th century. Only?

Of course, music historians know that there had been musicians in Vienna long before that date, that the Viennese have sung and danced for centuries, and that music was greatly appreciated in the church as well as at court. We could go back to the times of the "Minnesingers", the "troubadours", and mention Walther von der Vogelweide who "by the munificence of the splendid Court at Vienna graciously had permission to make music in Austria". But that would take us back to the 12th century, a little too far for us.

So, let us stay in the 15th century and with Emperor Maximilian I who, as an important German prince of the time, had his own court chapel. This means, of course, a band of musicians whom he selected and who provided such entertainment as the Emperor wished. Maximilian travelled extensively, but always with his musicians in tow as he was most anxious to be regarded throughout the world as a musical prince.

The year 1498 is important here, because we have documents from that year which give us an idea of the makeup of his "Kapelle" in Vienna. Although this was not a listing for a new music establishment, it does give us a definitive account of a group of musicians and singers, and so we take this date and the imperial document sufficiently seriously to date the beginning of the Hofmusikkapelle from it.

And that means, that—returning to the present for a moment—the latest date for the foundation of a musical institution in Vienna and at the Imperial Court that still exists and remains active to this very day was 1498. With rather minor changes it has survived all these centuries and, without any doubt, it is at the center of the city's musical life.

We shall have more to say about the continuous existence of the Court Chapel in the chapters on the great musical institutions of Vienna. Let us mention here, however, that today it includes the Vienna Choir Boys and members of the Vienna State Opera Chorus and Orchestra. The latter are not necessarily members of the Vienna Philharmonic, although most of them are. They perform masses on Sundays and church holidays during the season.

The Viennese themselves are occasionally slightly confused by this arrangement, for the Hofmusikkapelle performs music in the Court Chapel, but we must not confuse these two. The Court Chapel is the *place* where mass is sung, situated in the Wiedner Tract of the Hofburg, the oldest part of the Imperial Castle. The Hofmusikkapelle is a group of *musicians* who, since our date of 1498 performed at mass, but today perform only sacred music. The members of this group follow different occupations during the working day, much as they formerly did when in the service of the emperor as members of the Court Chapel. Remember that the singers and musicians of the Opera were, as long as there was an emperor, in the service and pay of His Majesty and had indeed to perform either at Court or at the Court Opera.

If anything has changed, it has to do with composers who formerly were members of the Court Chapel but who today are no longer permanent members. And with this we are back again in the year 1498.

Maximilian and his successors were interested not only in having fully trained singers and musicians, but also engaged the most outstanding composers of the time. It was not too difficult to acquire their services for the Emperor, as the fascination of the Imperial Court was so great that not only knights and money changers but also artists were attracted. Where else were they to find their glory, if not in the immediate neighborhood and munificence of the Emperor himself?

The list of musicians who were either the directors of the Court Chapel or who composed for this institution is impressive indeed. They were called to Vienna from all over Europe or simply came voluntarily to offer their services.

Music experts have some difficulty keeping track of this Court Chapel, for they have only the Imperial documents to guide them. So while they know that the Court Chapel travelled with the Emperor, they lack the documentary evidence to trace all the musicians associated with this institution. We can however assume a continuity of performers despite the Emperor's travels, though we can not prove it year by year in the documents.

Austria's rulers for centuries had their own "chapel" or musical establishment. The organization, which is still called the Hofmusikkapelle (Court Chapel) was first described in an imperial document dated 1498. The woodcut shows the choir boys of Emperor Maximilian I. Their successors today are known all over the world as the Vienna Choir Boys.

Music of the Emperors

We do not want to tell this story in full detail, but some background is necessary to understand the City of Music. All sorts of musicians were in the service of the Imperial Court, but early in the 16th century a separation of their services was inaugurated. The musicians who played for the Emperor as a symbol of his ecclesiastical role, were not identical to those who followed him into battle. The Emperor had, at all times, even in times of war, not only his court but his music with him as well. We know roughly the strength of these musical forces: In 1564 nearly 80 performers were members of the Court Chapel. But in addition there were pipers, trumpeters and drummers, always more than 16 and all holding the rank of officers.

All this is recounted at the beginning of this brief and, we hope, accessible musical history of Vienna, in order to give the reader some impression of the size of the "chapel" playing for the Emperor. On special occasions all the musicians in the service of the Emperor were gathered, so that one would often hear more than 100 players in one ensemble, which, with 16 powerful trumpeters, must have made a mighty sound, not simply the chirping of crickets, as some have imagined the music of those days.

The titles of "Chamber Musician", "Chamber Bass", even "Chamber Singer" were first introduced at the court of Maximilian II. This title, to this day, is given only to the best known singers of the State Opera and is one which they receive as a special honor. For it is an honorable tradition, well over 400 years old.

These ensembles always included some members of the nobility and even of the imperial household, which was a typical and unique Austrian practice. Although there was, here and there in history, a monarch or prince who made music himself, or even composed, Austria's House of Habsburg holds an impressive place in music history. The rulers in Vienna who either composed music, or performed in public, contributed markedly to its reputation as the Capital of Music. Vienna became the city where one came to expect a great love of and expertise in music, not only at the top of the social ladder, the Emperor himself, but at the bottom as well. It was this fact that brought the most important musicians of their time to Vienna and kept them there.

Now we turn to a few of the events that have become part and parcel of Viennese music history. At the wedding of Emperor Leopold I to Margareta Theresia of Spain, a horse ballet was performed on the square known today as Josefsplatz. The spectacle required a half a year's preparation, enormous technical skill and expense. Members of the imperial household were among the riders.

At that time a large opera house was located at that spot, a wooden structure designed by Burnacini for Emperor Leopold, with three galleries. On one occasion Marc Antonio Cesti's *Il Pomo d'Oro* was performed there, with 1,000 performers. The Emperor decided that the exclusive performance for the court was not sufficient for so grand a production so he invited the "populace" of Vienna to attend "repeat" performances. This opera house went up in flames after it was hit by gunfire during the second siege of Vienna by the Turks in 1683, but was reconstructed. Even at that time it was a matter of course that Vienna opera houses were promptly restored after war or fire had destroyed them.

Operas, *Singspiele,* ballets, oratorios and madrigals, written by Leopold I still exist.

Lodovico Burnacini built for Emperor Leopold I the first great opera house in Vienna in 1665, on the grounds of today's Burggarten (Castle Gardens). This wooden structure could accommodate several thousand people, but had to be pulled down when the Turks besieged Vienna in 1683 for the second time. Not only a privileged upper class but all of Vienna was admitted to these performances.

Those works were performed not only by the Court Chapel at his own court but elsewhere in the Empire as well. His contemporaries recognized them as good music, as we do, for in our time some of Leopold I's works continue to be performed in Vienna. Indeed, they do not give the impression of compositions by a socially privileged amateur.

Charles VI, Maria Theresia's father, followed the musical example of his predecessor. He called the German composer Gottlieb Muffat to the Imperial Court, enlarged his musical staff and wrote musical compositions himself. All of the latter have been lost.

Maria Theresia's thorough schooling included musical composition as well as singing lessons and she became an accomplished singer. During her time the Imperial Court in Vienna overflowed with famous names: Georg Christoph Wagenseil was one of her instructors; Florian Gassmann held an important musical post at her court; and Christoph Willibald Gluck, who had been called to Vienna and was a highly esteemed figure at the court, was responsible for the musical training of her children. These archdukes and archduchesses sang in his operas and tried, in their turn, to compose music. For Joseph II Antonio Salieri was retained as his music teacher. Joseph II, when Emperor himself, once took an opera singer's part simply for the fun of it. Leopold II, his successor, no great composer, played the harpsichord and retained, at least "pro forma", Wolfgang Amadeus Mozart in his services, although he remained attached to the famous Salieri and

Johann Josef Fux, born in Styria, was called to serve at the Court in Vienna. He is regarded as the great Austrian Baroque musician. His Gradus ad Parnassum *was for generations the most important musical text book. This engraving by Franz Ambros Dietel shows a scene from the opera* Angelina vincitrice di Alcina *that has been revived recently. His collaborator for this Viennese production of 1776 was Ferdinando Galli-Bibiena, a member of the famous Italian family of theater architects.*

his Italian taste in music. The continued existence of the Court Chapel has been a stimulant for the creation of many musical works and has encouraged the organization of other musical institutions important in our history.

It goes without saying that with rulers such as these the nobility, who regarded themselves as of nearly equal rank, felt compelled to foster music. It is equally clear that their musical interests were often passed on from one generation to the next; Viennese musicians have for centuries, almost to the present, greatly benefitted from the musical enthusiasm of the nobility as well as that of the "broader" masses. The works of Haydn and Beethoven, for example are, in their majority, associated with the bearers of titles of nobility. Their descendants still live in Vienna and often proudly remind us of the great deeds of their forefathers.

Yet the music enthusiast, the musically interested visitor to Vienna, need not despair because he cannot hum the music of Leopold I or knows next to nothing of the musical interests of Empress Maria Theresia. It will clearly suffice if he understands that in the then mighty empire music was one of the arts appreciated not only by the Emperor, but all classes of society. This understanding is a necessary precondition to an appreciation of why Vienna still occupies a place in music that has no parallel with any other city of the world.

Joseph Haydn

The life of most really great composers tends to follow a pattern that repeats itself again and again, if we do not dwell overly on details. We shall meet this pattern repeatedly in the course of this book but I shall not ignore qualities which distinguish one composer from another.

Joseph Haydn was born on March 31, 1732 at Rohrau in eastern Lower Austria. For years heart-rending stories of the poor and difficult circumstances from which he came were circulated. Only later was it learned that his father was a respected artisan, a professional and in a position to provide well for his family. Young Haydn is reported to have taken part in making music at home, but we know so little of his youth this cannot be proved. But clearly, the family must have had some inclination toward music or they would not have been willing to send two boys, Joseph and his brother Michael, who also became a composer, to Vienna to join the Court Chapel. By way of Hainburg, in eastern Austria, where Joseph received his first musical instruction, he joined the choir school (Kantorei) of St. Stephen's. He remained with this choir for nine years—boys did not lose their high voices until relatively late in those days.

Nine years with the choir of St. Stephen's meant nine years of thorough musical training and a close acquaintance with the music of his time as well as that theoretical and practical experience which a composer must receive in childhood. We shall see that all of Haydn's successors became practicing musicians early in life.

For the sake of accuracy and to correct a common misconception, let it be pointed out that while Haydn did sing at the time of Maria Theresia, it was not as a member of the Court Chapel but rather in the choir of the Cathedral of St. Stephen's. But his education was in no way less thorough there. He could no doubt have remained attached to St. Stephen's *Kantorei* after losing his boy's voice, but he was—it was said—a strong-willed young man and apparently one who was anxious to make a musical career.

After leaving the confines of the boys' choir Haydn lived in the old St. Michael's House (that still exists) and managed, by obtaining casual musical employment, to make enough money to both stay alive and further his musical training. Here, in the heart of Vienna, he had the best opportunities. Nicola Porpora, the famous voice and composition instructor, took him on as his assistant and offered, in return for faithful, if often humble services, further musical training. Pietro Metastasio, the respected Court poet and librettist, lived in the same house as young Haydn and saw to it that he had what even today is called the necessary good connections. As Porpora's apprentice Haydn was constantly in touch with aristocratic music lovers and, as Metastasio's protegé, in close touch with their tastes and preferences in music.

From 1759 on we can, so to speak, dispense with Haydn's life story, for at that time he accepted the position of music director at the court of a nobleman, Count Morzin at Lukavec near Pilsen, and later—1761—that of Kapellmeister with Prince Paul Esterházy at Eisenstadt.

Nearly 30 years later, starting in 1790, we find Haydn either on long and successful trips abroad or in Vienna. Despite this hiatus and his first position in Bohemia, and especially in the many years at Eisenstadt with the Esterházys, whose employ he did not leave as long as he lived, Haydn was above all a musician who might be called a Viennese.

A pencil drawing by George Dance, 1794. Haydn was at that time 62 years old (and for his time very old), and a world-famous musician who was very secure in his high position. In discussions and letters he could be at times very witty while at others, very offensive.

Joseph Haydn kept up a lively correspondence with his brother Michael all his life. Michael was active as a musician in Salzburg and may have had difficulties—as did many others—getting on with his sister-in-law. Michael never managed as a composer to get out of the shadow of his popular brother.

The residents of the city knew very well that there was a music director under whom Eisenstadt could easily compete with the Imperial Court as *the* music center.

In order to understand Haydn's position in the princely Esterházy household one must realize that the old social order, in which a musician's position was hardly above that of a lackey, was gradually changing. It was of course unthinkable at Haydn's time that the unbridgeable gap between a princely employer and an employee could be overlooked, so in a roster of Eisenstadt's residents one would have found Haydn among the servants. But it was equally true that his position, first as Second, soon thereafter as First Kapell-meister for a prince who thoroughly loved both music and pomp, was the envy of every musician in the empire.

Haydn's duties have been well described. He was to comply with his master's musical wishes, be prepared to perform his own or other music popular at the time and had to keep the musicians in readiness and fully rehearsed for this purpose. Moreover, he had to supervise the several princely opera houses, supervise rehearsals of new produc-tions, and compose operas himself, always keeping in mind the preferences of his master and the times.

But one can also look at Haydn's position from a different angle and conclude that Haydn possessed innumerable opportunities to test all that he composed by hearing it performed. As Kapellmeister of a prince who dearly loved music and as His Grace's opera director, he *heard* what he composed. Even today such an opportunity is hardly ever offered to a composer in such a generous manner as Haydn enjoyed throughout his life.

Haydn was required to compose a great deal of music, but he was also in a position to "order" a lot of it. As the director of the opera in the service of a rich prince intent on competing with the court in Vienna, he was able to establish a wide network of interna-tional connections. As the First Kapellmeister of a well equipped orchestra he was not only able to fulfill each and every one of his wishes, but also perform music by colleagues who quickly and gratefully reciprocated by putting his music on their programs.

As with all other composers Haydn's daily work schedule included writing such a quantity of notes as can hardly be imagined today. The catalogue of his works outnumbers all those of his contemporaries, even if one sweeps out everything that is in any way of doubtful authenticity. Yet, despite his enormous output, the real greatness and impor-tance of Haydn lies not in mere volume. He wrote many operas that are hardly known today, and if they are performed, only as excerpts. Though these fragments are exciting and interesting, Haydn's real greatness is to be found not in quantity alone.

His measure is to be found in the originality of his music. No two of his symphonies—and there are over a hundred of them, many of them far too little known—are alike. When listening to a broad range of his symphonies, we note with excitement that "Papa" Haydn, as he is sometimes condescendingly called, composed with more daring and experimented more widely than any other composer. Which in turn leads one to recognize a characteristic sign of genius: A great composer refuses to confine himself to the rules he learned and observed in his apprenticeship and while maturing, but stretches them in all directions and not infrequently breaks them outright to put in place new rules that soon are accepted by his contemporaries.

Haydn wrote vast quantities of chamber music because the princes whom he served were themselves practicing musicians and ever desired new works to play. Who was to supply them, if not their own Kapellmeister whom they had employed and were paying?

Haydn incorporated into his chamber music and his symphonies "effects" that have become a virtual hallmark—unexpected harmonic twists, or the famous "surprise" on the kettledrum during the quiet introduction to a symphony. There is much musical humor which we know the composer intended as such. Most likely he did not hold a high opinion of his listeners and wanted to rouse them by providing the unexpected or humorous. He was probably also given to some malice: we know from his letters that he was not at all a quiet and humble musician, but at times quick-tempered and quite self-confident—a composer who criticized competitors sharply and who insisted on being recognized as somebody very special.

And—after all—that is what he was. When Prince Nicolas died in 1790 and his successor turned out to be less interested in music, Haydn moved to Vienna and even accepted concert appearances in London, though he officially remained in the service of Their Lordships, the princes of Esterházy. Loyalty and wisdom prevented him from giving up his firm ties to the princely house. Open to new ideas, to the world around him, he sought and maintained ties with fellow composers. In these contacts and the wider world of Vienna and London he found new inspiration that he quickly absorbed and utilized. From 1790 until 1792 and from 1794 until 1795 he was in London where he composed not only the famous "London Symphonies", but also quartets and trios, and learned that one could write oratorios. In his old age, he wrote *The Creation* (1790) and *The Seasons,* (1801) works that are today as inspiring as they were at their first performance.

These oratorios were greeted with such enthusiasm at their first performances that one can disperse with the legend of the misunderstood genius, for Joseph Haydn experienced during his lifetime what we would call today international fame. He was asked by patrons throughout Europe to compose for them, his work was performed across the continent, he was adored in Vienna and was almost unable to fend off students.

Here we should turn to the matter of Haydn's relationship to Mozart and Beethoven, of which most music lovers have heard but which is not well understood from Haydn's point of view. The successful musician, Haydn, admired throughout Europe, met Mozart when the latter was still a child. He later became an important friend when Mozart decided, against the will of his father, to move to Vienna leaving the service of the Prince Archbishop of Salzburg. The young composer dedicated some of his great string quartets to Haydn. When Mozart's father came to Vienna Haydn confirmed to him that no greater composer was known to him than Wolfgang Amadeus Mozart. He was in London when Mozart died.

Beethoven, who had been sent to Vienna so he could receive instruction from Haydn, unfortunately never established a close relationship with the aging man. Haydn had become moody and vain and was most likely simply not the best teacher for Beethoven. Haydn felt insulted by him and abruptly terminated instruction upon learning that Beethoven was also taking lessons from Johann Georg Albrechtsberger. Furthermore Haydn was by this time no longer interested in working with individual students. He was more interested in teaching brief "master classes" for young musicians who flocked to Vienna from all of Europe, and in being regarded as the pre-eminent teacher of the musical world.

The contacts of the three "great ones" of Viennese Classicism—often illustrated by quotations which have no real foundation in truth—thus were of varying closeness. Haydn's contacts with the young genius of Mozart were those of a recognized master who ungrudgingly acknowledged the greatness of a young and endearing successor to his own fame. On the other hand, Haydn no longer could establish such rapport with the young Beethoven.

While much of Haydn's work fell into obscurity in subsequent generations, much on the other hand has never lost its place in the world of music. Haydn's Masses remain the work of a genius and are as popular today as they were on their first day of performance. They were all "commissioned," to be performed for the first time on special occasions but have never disappeared from the liturgical repertoire. His chamber music

Joseph Haydn—here as a silhouette together with Nancy Storace and Catarina Cavalieri— was an unhappily married composer,—a not exceptional state of affairs. In the course of time it has been forgotten that he enjoyed the friendship and admiration of many women, including singers, to compensate for his unfortunate marriage. The musician Nancy Storace was among them as was Catarina Cavalieri. The latter was one of the most popular singers of her time, a favorite student of Antonio Salieri in Vienna. She had a first-class position, singing the leading roles in works of Haydn and Mozart.

was eagerly sought after by music lovers and remains to this day in the repertoire of all musicians, whether amateur or professional. His "folk song" commissioned as a simple hymn, became and remained the national anthem of Austria, well into this century. That, in 1945, Austria abandoned the *Deutschlandied* as a national anthem is understandable, and that Austrians still love Haydn's hymn today is beyond doubt.

During the last years of his life Joseph Haydn was a lonely but much sought-after gentleman living in a Vienna suburb. He was called upon by a host of notable visitors and devoted musicians. His "round number" (i.e. 60, 70) birthdays were the occasions for festive performances of his works at the conclusion of which the Viennese aristocracy fêted him. He spent the last few months of his life sitting in an easy chair and silently handed visitors a calling card he had specially printed for this purpose. The card bore the text of one of his songs which read in part: "Gone is all my strength . . ." It must have been heart-rending to see the old master declare his own resignation in such a way.

On the 27th of March 1808, *The Creation* was once more performed in his honor in the Festival Hall of the University. Antonio Salieri was the conductor and the leading performers of Vienna played. Salieri's role is especially significant, as he was not only one of the most important musicians in Vienna but at least as importantly represented that which is referred to as tradition. And since a chapter in this brief book cannot be devoted to Salieri, one has to mention him whenever it is possible. He had played the harpsichord at the first performance of *The Creation;* taught Beethoven; was suspected of having poisoned Mozart; was Schubert's teacher and a member of the Society of Friends of Music, an institution still of great importance and thoroughly characteristic of the City of Music.

Haydn lay dying when Napoleon made his victorious entry into Vienna. Napoleon ordered that straw be spread on the pavement before Haydn's house, so that the noise of his cavalry riding past would not disturb the dying genius.

Haydn's devoted servant and music copyist, Johann Elssler, was responsible for the sobriquet since associated with the composer by referring to him soon after his death as "Papa" Haydn. Elssler was later to father the dancer Fanny Elssler, who became the close friend of Friedrich von Gentz, one of Metternich's favorites. It has been rumored that Fanny Elssler had a love affair with the Duke of Reichstadt, Napoleon's son. Clearly even at that time very close personal relationships were established between musical families

and the highest social and political circles. Imperial Vienna was after all only a village, as the saying goes, when one examines closely social relationships between important figures. The villagers in such stories were named Haydn, Napoleon, Elssler, Gentz, and Metternich, people not without historical significance.

Haydn's estate, inventoried after his death on May 31, 1809, was considerable. His biographers noted that at the time of Haydn's death only 3% of Vienna's population left more than 10,000 guilders, while Haydn's fortune was valued at 35,000 guilders. So, the well-loved and widely recognized master, a man who had worked hard all his life as a musician, died a rich man.

Had he been happy? Of his marriage of 40 years, we know little. Maria Anna Kellner, daughter of a Viennese wigmaker, bore him no children and is said to have caused him some bitterness. But after her death Haydn neither sought another partner nor blossomed in society so we must assume that he had become accustomed to living with a wife who most likely did not understand him. It is rumored that he had another love late in life, a doctor's wife, Marianne von Genzinger, who was greatly admired by the aging Haydn. But it is hardly necessary to dwell on this matter.

Haydn was a man of considerable stature. As a composer of world-wide repute he was entitled to a splendid funeral, attended not only by music lovers and high officials, but also by Napoleon's officers. The fact that his grave was later despoiled and his skull removed for "scientific purposes", as was said, is part and parcel of the criminal history of music. In a round-about way the skull later came into the possession of the Society of Friends of Music in Vienna and was restored to his grave at Eisenstadt only in our time.

His music lost some of its popularity soon after his death. The numerous operas were quickly forgotten, his symphonies were generally underrated and published in unreliable editions. Only his greatly admired chamber music remained on the music stands, in the houses of generations of music lovers, without interruption. And the oratorios are, like his masses, still performed regularly.

It was only in the 20th century that Haydn found his archivist: Anthony von Hoboken first compiled a catalogue of all of Haydn's works, but a generation of researchers is still hard at work and their task not yet completed. Compositions thought lost continue to come to light. On the other hand some works ascribed to Haydn have been found to be spurious. So the standard Hoboken catalogue still is being revised.

19

And what of Haydn's influence? Modern interpreters of his music recognize that this music was inspired by a great genius and well ahead of its time, so increasing attention is being devoted to it. The characterizations of his work, even those created by prominent musicians of the 19th century, are out of fashion. Haydn's music is no longer just lovely, no longer only playful. Today we see and hear in it genuine grandeur and inspiration and, no doubt, it still possesses "potential" for future exploration.

Many admirers who visited the aging Haydn in his Vienna home described this scene: The aging composer received them in a friendly manner, but was rather withdrawn from reality, handing them this calling-card printed for such occasions. It was at this time that the expression "Papa Haydn" became firmly established, not at all appropriate for the revolutionary music of Haydn, thus doing him and it a considerable disservice. (The words below the music say: "Gone is all my strength, old and weak am I" and above it; "Molto adagio"—very slow.)

Wolfgang Amadeus Mozart

Again and again we read and hear of the boundless admiration that makes it impossible to understand Wolfgang Amadeus Mozart in any way other than by silent, admiring veneration. Certainly, there is some truth in this view. But some have pointed to ways by which one can adore and at the same time understand this remarkable composer.

Born January 27, 1756 in Salzburg, the son of a busy and well respected musician, Mozart remains to this day the most famous of all child prodigies. Presented by his father as the youngest keyboard player not only in Salzburg but the entire world, Mozart experienced a strange and most unusual childhood. When dealing with a child prodigy and the inevitable difficulties attendant thereto, some observations are in order.

At the time the Mozarts were travelling, "child prodigies" were not all that unusual, in fact musical children were regularly presented only to lose their appeal and be quickly forgotten. As a child Mozart was required by his father to practice both on instruments and composition for a number of hours each day. But the boy's native enthusiasm for making music far exceeded his father's expectations: Mozart was not one of those drilled child prodigies or *Wunderkinder* but rather managed to produce *Wunder*, miracles, by virtue of his own interests and enthusiasms.

Curiously, while we are writing of Viennese music we must deal with musicians whose origins were not Viennese. The Mozarts hailed from Augsburg and even Wolfgang Amadeus Mozart was not an "Austrian", having been born in Salzburg, whose ruling prince was the Prince Archbishop. The whole of the archbishopric of Salzburg had not yet by this time become one of the Austrian monarch's hereditary possessions. The violin player, Leopold Mozart, enjoyed a secure income as an employee in the Prince Archbishop's service and moved in the center of the prosperous citizens of Salzburg among whom he sought and made many friends and patrons for himself and his family. Yet he has been presented by history in as false a light as was his son. It is true that he presented his daughter, "Nannerl", and his beloved son, called "Wolferl" in many biographies, as small curiosities which led to a lifestyle for them that can only be compared to that of today's circus children. Yet he acquainted his son, wonderfully gifted not only with dexterous fingers but an innate sense of music, with all the serious music (as Leopold knew it) of his time.

We possess very detailed information about the "tours" of the Mozarts, for Father Mozart incessantly wrote detailed reports of successes and intrigues. But one must learn how to read his letters: they not infrequently either embellished successes or treated difficulties tearfully. Travel was as difficult for the Mozarts as it was for everybody at that time—and they sought their public wherever it could be found or hoped for. So the two children occasionally performed in inns and amazed audiences of humbler station. They repeatedly had to perform with blindfold eyes or to employ similar senseless tricks. But they were also introduced to aristocratic circles wherever possible and so performed before audiences which were sometimes fully appreciative of the Mozart artists, sometimes very bored. More importantly, however, they were also introduced to professional colleagues who quickly recognized that Wolfgang Amadeus Mozart especially possessed an unusual gift surpassing other child prodigies.

The most famous of these tours lasted more than three years and took them through

Mozart has been described to us in various ways, but there is only one unfinished portrait of him in which he is not shown in an idealized fashion. Here is an etching by Giovanni Antonio Sasso from about 1786, showing Mozart at the fortepiano.

Germany, Belgium, France, England, and the Netherlands. It brought them not only money but also great fame. Among the most famous contemporaries who heard little Mozart in the 1760s was Johann Wolfgang Goethe. The best known and most often reported meeting with the world of the aristocracy was, no doubt, the little musician's appearance before Maria Theresia. The chroniclers all report that the Empress was delighted with the precocious instrumentalist, but few of them note that later she found little of interest in the mature composer.

The most significant experiences, however, were those the 14-year-old Mozart gained in Italy, during a tour most cleverly and carefully prepared by the father. It was there that he absorbed that abundance of musical impressions and practical experience so important for his own composing which he could in all probability not have gathered elsewhere. Italy, the country of music, fully accepted the miracle of Mozart and heaped upon the boy not only the honors due to him but, only with slightly more reticence, gave him commissions. Above all else, Mozart eagerly and thoroughly absorbed the great musical tradition of that country.

Music historians have been able to identify Mozart's personal style even in his earliest compositions with the unfortunate consequence that we are now expected to accept and admire even the lesser works of an incomprehensibly large oeuvre with enthusiasm. When listening to the music of the boy Mozart, or one or the other of the early operas, we most likely arrive at the absolutely acceptable verdict that while good it is not extraordinary music. Mozart, the child, composed in keeping with the taste of his times, to which the paternal teacher had no objection. What we call Mozart's originality and particularly what, with a shrug of the shoulders, is styled "genius" or "inspired mastery" came only with increasing maturity. Anyone arriving at another view is at best engaging in indiscriminating adulation.

As a young man, Mozart was much in demand as a virtuoso pianist and as a composer. He was never comfortable in the confined atmosphere of Salzburg following his truly turbulent and adventuresome childhood years. The position of a musician on a fixed salary, dependent on his princely patron, in this case the Prince Archbishop, was, no doubt, not only stultifying, but too menial and too boring as well. His reported insolence is sometimes interpreted as an indomitable urge for freedom, as a musician's revolt in an age of revolution. But a more personal, seemingly simpler explanation can be advanced. Here was a gifted musician, not yet 20, whom the most illustrious princes and most distinguished musicians had admired when he was a child, yet who in Salzburg and so near to Italy was so weighed down by the menial duties and exacting demands of the Archbishop that he could not realize his musical capacities. A position at the Imperial Court and life in the capital seemed the only reasonable option. His provocative behavior, aimed at being "kicked out" of Salzburg and received in Vienna with open arms, originated, no doubt, not from a love for that city nor its inhabitants, but simply from a desire to move into one of Europe's cultural centers.

We do know that Mozart repeatedly made plans to move to several other cities and that he would have accepted, without hesitation, a prominent position at a comparable princely court elsewhere. The music capital, Vienna, was lucky enough to receive him only because other invitations were neither serious nor sufficiently concrete. So it was only fortunate circumstance that the man from Salzburg maintained a life-long connection with Vienna.

After a "row" with his master in Salzburg which has become part of history, (the Archbishop literally had him booted out of his Vienna palace, because he refused to return to Salzburg) young Mozart settled down in Vienna and thus became, without intending to do so, the first major free-lance composer of repute. He never abandoned his hope of landing an acceptable well-paid position, but it is clear that he never truly tried to acquire the necessary "prestige" to do so. That is to say, he did little to cultivate the airs and connections necessary to become a court Kapellmeister. He taught piano lessons, gave concerts of his own music as a virtuoso on that instrument; married Konstanze Weber against his father's will (even this was easier in Vienna than under close supervision of his family), and composed *The Abduction from the Seraglio,* all in the season of 1781/1782.

His social contacts in Vienna certainly included all the important people of the city, including Haydn and the music lover and scholar Van Swieten, as well as well-to-do citizens who were Free Masons and therefore "brothers" of the composer. His contacts included not only those who had something to do with music and the theater, but also the general public who, in his view, were to support and back him.

His marriage was a chapter apart, and again it fits the pattern that marks most great composers: Like Haydn, who for over 40 years battled through life with a wife who had

Konstanze Mozart has become part of history as the wife of Mozart whom he had married against the wishes of his domineering father. She is now judged to have been an "inconstant," flighty person, a not very understanding wife standing at the side of an endangered genius. But she also was the first widow of a composer to cultivate the reputation of her late husband by making his works and biography her concern. This lithograph from the year 1783 appears in the first biography of Mozart, published by her second husband.

little understanding of art, Mozart had in his beloved Konstanze neither a faithful nor an understanding companion. She bore him six children, of whom only two sons survived early childhood, not uncommon at that time. She not only took whatever money came in, but also deprived him of any appearance of decency and honor by entertaining intimate acquaintances outside marriage, so openly that even musicologists note her behavior— but we need not dwell on so sordid a matter. *The Marriage of Figaro,* Mozart's first opera not composed for a patron, was first performed in Vienna in 1786. But it was in Prague that it met with such overwhelming success that Mozart subsequently composed *Don Giovanni,* first performed in 1787, for this city so appreciative of his music—as well as the "Prague" Symphony (K504).

　　Of the many Mozart stories now popularized in plays and films presented worldwide one is almost true: His *Marriage of Figaro* cost Mozart the support of the Viennese nobility who felt that Beaumarchais' text, even in Da Ponte's version, was both an insult and an impertinence. This reaction resulted in the loss of any further opportunity Mozart had to be music tutor to the sons and daughters of nobility and to give concerts under

Hieronymus Löschenkohl cut many series of silhouettes; some of which later appeared as playing cards. The actors in Mozart's Le Nozze di Figaro *were sufficiently popular as singers of the first order to sit for Löschenkohl.*

their patronage. The fees for such lessons and concerts would have allowed him a comfortable life. The popularity of Mozart's music was, of course, not diminished by the unwillingness of an entire class of society to associate with him. Countless arrangements of his operas for various instruments give proof of the continuing popularity of his work as does the fact that melodies from his *Figaro* were whistled and sung everywhere, as was done later with greatly successful operettas, which proves the good taste of the broad public at least.

It is well to keep in mind the qualities Mozart possessed and which carried him to the first rank of composers. Like Haydn, he had the reputation of being an unimaginably productive musician. We know that he loved partying and attended a great many social and musical functions, so we can only be amazed at the quantity of music that he must have written, day in and day out. And of course quantity is a matter quite apart from quality, but the quantity alone is really astonishing. Indeed modern research established that the sheer bulk of Mozart's oeuvre cannot be expected from even a mere copyist.

In 1788 Mozart composed his last three great symphonies, in E-flat major, G minor and C major (the "Jupiter"), but they were not by a long shot all that Mozart wrote in that year. In 1789 he was again on tour, yet composed some string quartets for King Frederick William II of Prussia at Potsdam, among other works. 1790 is the year of *Così fan tutte,* the

Emanuel Schikaneder encouraged Mozart to write The Magic Flute *for his suburban theater, thus ensuring success, not only for the composer, but for himself as the first Papageno as well. He sold his illustrated libretto for the opera to an enthusiastic public. Mozart invited his colleague Antonio Salieri to one of the first repeat performances and delightedly reported Salieri's "Bravo" calls.*

opera of shifting love affairs, purportedly based on a true occurrence. Soon after Mozart's death *Così* underwent the not unusual fate of being underestimated. Only in the age of psychoanalysis, though without the cooperation of any psychoanalyst, was the work resurrected as a masterpiece.

The last year of Mozart's life, 1791, probably best characterizes and sums up his genius. He composed the coronation opera *La Clemenza di Tito* which gave new life to an old form of opera. He then went on to write *The Magic Flute* at the request of the director of a suburban theater, Emanuel Schikaneder, but in so doing perfected a new type of opera that had existed before only in tentative form. This *genre* is called "Zauberstück" (magic play) and was later used in romantic opera containing incidents of magic and bearing a humanitarian message. In addition to these major works he began the composition of his *Requiem.* An anonymous patron, long since identified, had ordered the work but received it only after Mozart's death, completed by his student, Franz Xaver Süssmayr.

Legends of all kinds are entwined around Mozart's death on December 5, 1791. As far as is humanly possible they have all been demystified. Salieri did not poison him: Mozart died of a kidney malfunction. He did not die in utter poverty, for his friends among the Free Masons had loaned him amounts that could only be called substantial even by composers living today. Nor were the circumstances of his funeral as melodramatic as the stories of decades would have it. That his coffin was not taken out to the cemetery in solemn procession was customary at the time. That a thunder storm was going on at the time has been proved incorrect by the daily meteorologic records. And finally that he was just "dug in" is also basically untrue, for it was one of those simple funerals officially decreed by the Emperor. The Viennese public who have always loved pomp and circumstance soon made known their disfavor, and the decree was rescinded. The city regretted that Mozart was not one of those who had been honored by a large and elaborate funeral, usual both before and following a short period surrounding the master's death.

But Mozart was never forgotten. His widow, who remarried, was not only frequently called upon by musicians, but also witnessed her dead husband's spreading fame. Goethe undertook the writing of a second part of the *Magic Flute* and declared that Mozart alone could have composed music suitable for his *Faust*. Music lovers from all over Europe made their pilgrimages to Vienna and to Salzburg, even invading the private life of Mozart's sister "Nannerl" in Salzburg. Places somehow connected with his life were turned into public memorials. Mozart's only surviving son, Franz Xaver Wolfgang, who preferred to sign himself W. A. Mozart, was the guest of honor at the dedication of the first Mozart monument in Salzburg. Mozart's birthplace assumed for itself the right to be called the "Mozart City" and endeavored to quash evidence that Mozart had left it in a huff. Vienna was hardly able to counter this campaign for while the city had been the seat of Mozart's effort to realize his life's ambitions, it had done little to help him realize them.

No musical era "after Mozart" has set forth any justifiable grounds from which to criticize or improve upon his genius. Subsequent periods have brought all manner of distortions through new interpretations—particularly in the case of *Don Giovanni* which has been debased with new and strange added finales. Nor have the changing tastes of the times been kinder, offering new meanings and interpretations and seeking justification in the story of Mozart's life.

But throughout, one point has held fast: Mozart was the most universal, most comprehensive example of musical genius that has ever lived among us. Even interpreters straining the hardest to be startling, and the most critical musicologists finally emerge from their exercises with amazed and loving admiration.

Antonio Salieri (1750–1825) was one of the most interesting and, at the same time, most misrepresented personalities of music history. Student and friend of Gluck, he was a close colleague of Haydn, an important teacher for Beethoven and Schubert and altogether a leading figure in the Viennese music world. And yet, stories continue to circulate that he poisoned Mozart.

Ludwig van Beethoven

People everywhere, when speaking or writing about the Viennese Classic period, refer to the "Great Three," meaning Haydn, Mozart and Beethoven. Strictly speaking, this is a loose formulation, for Ludwig van Beethoven, who received lessons from Haydn and was tutored briefly by Mozart, in his maturity had left far behind him what is meant by "classicism," having become one of the chief representatives of "romanticism"—a musical era—which, without him, could not be imagined.

All labels in music tend to be superficial, vague and inaccurate. And yet, we had best not object to them too strenuously, for it is after all possible and indeed necessary to see Haydn, Mozart, and Beethoven as an over-life-size grouping of immortal musicians in Vienna.

Ludwig van Beethoven, too, was a "Wunderkind", a child prodigy, who had visited Vienna for a short while before he finally settled in the city for the rest of his life. Beethoven, too, seriously thought of establishing himself elsewhere after he had acquired a generally recognized reputation in Vienna, and might have done so had he been offered a promising opportunity. So even in his case Vienna was simply lucky, because it offered the best teachers, the most alert promoters, and musical opportunities offered by no other city. Bonn can certainly claim to be Beethoven's birthplace and draw honor upon itself on this account, but Vienna, its suburbs and its surroundings will always point out that the "Titan" lived and suffered and worked here.

Ludwig van Beethoven, born on December 17, 1770, the child of a singer in the Court Chapel of Bonn, was tutored by his father, in conscious awareness of the child prodigy Mozart, to play the piano like a virtuoso and to perform in public under the pretense that he was younger than he really was. But Johann van Beethoven was not as good a musician as Leopold Mozart, nor were the first teachers that he chose for his son able to draw from the boy what the child Mozart was able to produce in his first own compositions and extraordinary public appearances. Beethoven was nine years old before he encountered a teacher equal to his native abilities. Christian Gottlieb Neefe, who gave young Beethoven piano lessons as well as training in music theory, was an excellent pedagogue and laid the foundation for the good general education in music that the child prodigy Beethoven possessed, when at long last he was presented to the public.

It was also Neefe who as a respected member of the Court Chapel of the Elector of Cologne, Maximilian Francis, managed to present young Beethoven as a talent worthy of attention, an undertaking in which Father Beethoven had not been successful. In 1787 the Bonn nobility sent Beethoven to Vienna, the Mecca of music, to receive instruction from Mozart himself. This first venture was cut short by the illness and death of Beethoven's mother after which his father became the "victim of drink," as such problems are euphemistically described. The young musician returned home as he had become the only money earning member of the family.

In 1792 his father died and once more the means were collected to send Beethoven to Vienna. This time he was to study with Haydn. We know that Beethoven did so for a short while but little came of it. The aging master and the budding composer were unable to establish real rapport. The fact that Beethoven sought and found other teachers behind Haydn's back further annoyed this most famous composer of his time. But it brought

Young Ludwig van Beethoven around 1786 as Court Organist to the Prince Bishop of Cologne. Soon after he was sent to Vienna where he gained a reputation as a young virtuoso and wild genius. The fascination he managed to exert on his noble protectors did not diminish even when, as a result of his failing hearing, he neglected his appearance and stormed through Vienna, having gained the reputation of extreme shyness.

Beethoven in contact with Johann Schenk and Johann Georg Albrechtsberger, two good teachers and musicians whose works are still performed, as well as the ubiquitous Antonio Salieri, the composer behind the great composers. This made possible not only the hoped-for musical training but also Beethoven's first major public appearances in Vienna.

What sort of an image did the young Beethoven create in Vienna? He was "wild", he was a foreigner, and he was recognized by the nobility as a budding genius. What he composed and what he performed was wholly within the style of the time, and the way he performed was exciting and extraordinarily brilliant. In his way, he was and remained until his death an exotic man—he never tried to change his accent, never employed the softer Viennese intonation and remained an obstinate "German" who could not take root here.

At the same time, he knew very well how one had to conduct oneself as a musician.

In his letters to his noble patrons he adopted the submissive tone required at the time, which today sounds to us like that of a lackey but was needed just as are certain turns of phrase and of address today. The young musician, wild and interesting as he was, whose progress was closely followed in Bonn and Cologne, and who became a real worry to his Viennese noble protectors, was respected and beloved.

But it is the same story all over again: legends of the lonely and completely misunderstood young genius are simply old wives tales. We can confidently assert that the musical world recognized and paid full honor to the young composer virtually from the day of his entrance into Vienna. The appearances of this young virtuoso, Beethoven, were sensational and brought him enough money that he was able to help support his younger brother and could live and compose without financial worries.

No doubt he would have conducted his social life in other ways had there been no early signs of the illness that was to separate him from the world around him in such a tragic manner. His deafness set in early and progressed slowly but inexorably.

It must be noted that he never completely lost his hearing. Until his death he was able to catch snatches of music and to understand what was shouted at him. But he did feel isolated by virtue of this serious impairment, incurable at the time. And let us mention another detail: It is due to Beethoven's deafness that we possess those numerous notebooks used by him to conduct conversations, that have been pored over and commented upon repeatedly. What a scandal it was then when recent scholarly studies revealed that large parts of these conversation notebooks had been falsified by a devoted pupil of Beethoven's. Thus posterity, largely because earlier music historians had taken them to be reliable source materials, arrived at a Beethoven picture which was not entirely correct.

Beethoven's impairment prompted one of the most moving documents known in the world of music, the so-called "Heiligenstadt Testament" of October 1802, written by Beethoven while he lived in that Vienna suburb. It was intended for his brothers, as both a crying out against the injustice of the world and as a will. Here we meet a successful musician, full of expectations, but afraid of losing both his hearing and his life at an early age. Since then all music lovers have agreed that it is a testament to Beethoven's suffering and moral greatness.

It is clear that this creeping impairment significantly contributed to Beethoven's difficulty in establishing close relationships with his fellow men. Even more certainly, it underlay his difficulties in establishing and maintaining a relationship with the several women he came to adore. We know that he was in love repeatedly, and developed new hopes that he was repeatedly forced to abandon. We still do not know if he was, at least for short moments, a happy man.

In the early 1800s Beethoven was, at any rate, a respected musician whose works were published and performed, whose concerts were well attended and whose students were well situated. With his ballet *The Creatures of Prometheus* he had made his first contact with the theater. His symphonies were considered inspired continuations in this genre.

In 1804 he finished the *Eroica* which was not only a musical masterpiece but one of those standard works which maintain their uninterrupted popularity thanks not only to a fitting and effective title, but also to the fact that we know how the title was chosen. Full of youthful enthusiasm, Beethoven planned to dedicate this symphony to Napoleon, but changed his mind in disgust when Napoleon had himself crowned Emperor, thus betraying the ideals of the French Revolution. These events have, however, nothing to do with the musical quality of the work. But it is an undeniable fact that mankind does not rally to quality alone. When a suitable, inspiring title is found for a symphony, an opera, or even a string quartet, the fame of the work grows immeasurably faster, a factor which we will note again when we come to speak of Schubert.

"Beethoven taking a walk" is the caption of this famous drawing by Joseph Daniel Böhm, ca. 1823. It is an unsentimental picture of the composer who would wander through Vienna and its environs in any kind of weather. Contemporaries called him a "composer of nature." The term was also applied to Schubert and carried not altogether flattering connotations.

In 1805 *Fidelio* was produced at the Theater an der Wien, which continues today as a music theater; its appearance has hardly changed. The opera was a failure on its first performance. In 1806 the second version of the opera was performed—also unsuccessfully. In 1814 at long last, this work the uniqueness and very special importance of which in music history no one can deny, had its third and this time successful premiere in Vienna.

Between these dates, however, lies 1808, the year in which Beethoven received a serious offer from Kassel. The consequence of this offer was that he was able to negotiate with his patrons an unparalleled understanding that enabled him to live and compose in complete financial security. A document signed in January 1809 by Archduke Rudolph and the Princes Francis Joseph Lobkowitz and Ferdinand Kinsky guaranteed the composer a yearly stipend which was solely to ensure his continued residence in Vienna.

It is really of little matter that the sum originally stipulated was quickly found to be insufficient due to inflation, and that this led to litigation with the heirs of the patrons. What is important is that these patrons, members of the aristocracy, recognized the genius of Beethoven and gave proof of their regard not only for the composer, but for Vienna, by not letting a composer of the rank of Ludwig van Beethoven emigrate to any other court. And they put their money behind their regard.

At the time of the Congress of Vienna, 1814/15, when rulers of Europe assembled in Vienna in order to deal with the redistribution of political power, they also wished to enjoy, between negotiating sessions, the amusements and entertainments that the imperial capital had to offer. With them also came those merely seeking to enjoy the same entertainments. Beethoven then was a master whom "the whole world" revered. His most important works had been completed, but the greatest excitement was associated with a few compositions commissioned for special occasions, such as the "symphonic poem" (although this term had not yet been invented) "Wellington's Victory." With the help of trumpets, cannons and appropriate national anthems it described not only the battle scenes but the ultimate triumph of the field marshal over Napoleon's armies. Beethoven's eight symphonies and many overtures were performed, but this extravagant showpiece was the true crowd pleaser.

But again we have to be careful in our perceptions. The kings and princes who came to Vienna were aware of Beethoven's fame and were ready to acknowledge him as an extraordinary musician. Yet Beethoven was no celebrity in today's sense of the word. The conventional boundaries of social standing were still intact. It would still have been unthinkable to establish intimate friendships between classes: There always remained that unbridgeable gap between "patron" and Beethoven that both parties accepted as a matter of fact.

Several years before, in 1812, Beethoven met with Goethe. The episode then occurred when, as they encountered the Emperor and his party, Goethe politely stepped aside and raised his hat as was customary when meeting royalty, while Beethoven walked straight on, so self-confident that he refused to observe such deference. His behavior caused such a sensation that the story was recounted halfway around Europe. The "prince of poets" expressed his disapproval although he remained convinced of the composer's greatness. We do not hear of similar episodes at the time of the Vienna Congress, only stories about the secret police spying on Beethoven and seeking to portray him as a dangerous firebrand.

Beethoven, by now almost completely deaf, became more and more isolated from his surroundings; at the same time, the interest of the public in his works waned. The years after 1815 were less steeped in glory for Beethoven than those of the Vienna Congress. He moved with ever greater frequency from apartment to apartment, from the city into new quarters in the country or in the suburbs; he often maintained two apartments at the same time. He had arguments with his friends with whom he could communicate only with the aid of the conversation notebooks. He worried about his nephew Karl, whose guardian he had become. He even went to court with his sister-in-law whom he despised, and whose son Karl Beethoven sought to bring up in accordance with *his* ideas; he worried so seriously and so clumsily about the boy that Karl attempted suicide as a result.

We may view Beethoven in those years as an eccentric, an aging bohemian of world-wide fame who completely neglected his appearance, whose genius was beyond doubt but who struck what we call "normal people" as intimidating or disgusting. At the same time, we must keep in mind that the musical world of Vienna knew who Beethoven was and tried to maintain contact or even work with the master. Franz Grillparzer was only one of the poets who would have been gratified to write a libretto for a second Beethoven opera. Beethoven did not compose another, beginning work instead in 1817 on his *Missa solemnis* and his Ninth Symphony. Both remain towering, inexhaustible masterpieces; they were first performed in 1823 and 1824. The last four great piano sonatas were finished in 1822. After that the last string quartets were the only major compositions, works that even today are regarded as difficult, that is, not entirely entertaining.

Slowly and strangely those last few years passed. The composer, now suspicious of the world around him and estranged from it, entertained a lively correspondence with his publishers, and accepted commissions from abroad. He had a "confidant" in Anton Schindler who not only partly falsified the conversation notebooks but also distorted Beethoven's image in his biography, accepted for many years as authentic. All this was done not for the purpose of changing the master's image but in order to place Schindler in a favorable light.

When Beethoven died on March 26, 1827, Vienna fully appreciated what a master had passed away. It is said that 20,000 people attended his funeral. Franz Grillparzer wrote the funeral oration. Franz Schubert, among other composers, was present at the graveside. He had met Beethoven only once and was to survive him by but one year.

Neither Beethoven nor his works fell into disfavor or oblivion. His compositions were seen as pointing to the future, and composers of the next generation looked to him as their model. Richard Wagner was not alone in considering himself authorized to preserve Beethoven's work in a "contemporary" style. Up to the time of Gustav Mahler conductors took it upon themselves to alter the instrumentation of the symphonies, because they were of the opinion that Beethoven, being deaf, had intended "more" than he was able to express with the means at his disposal. As time went on, bringing about improvements in instruments, players and conductors incorporated these into Beethoven's scores. The debate as to whether this practice is justifiable is not yet concluded.

That every generation presented him differently cannot be supported by this argument. In contrast to Mozart, Beethoven had reached his zenith as a giant, a Titan, a hero while still alive, and this image has never changed in music circles.

Franz Schubert

We have already mentioned the name of the great exception among Vienna's great composers: Franz Schubert, born on 31 January 1797 in a Vienna suburb, the musician who not only did not have to move to the city, but also never had any desire to leave it. The true-born, the genuine "Viennese."

His father was an elementary school teacher and therefore had some musical interests, for at that time some basic musical instruction was part of the curriculum. A school teacher felt compelled to prove his qualifications by showing that, above all, he was musical. Schubert's father and all his family were, according to contemporary and present-day standards, poor. They lived in a rented home in the suburb, marked by crowded conditions; instruction and living quarters were concentrated in a single room. Infant and childhood mortality was a terrible scourge of the time. Franz Schubert was the 11th child and experienced, as his mother became pregnant again and again, the death of brothers and sisters. He was given to understand that this was the natural course of events and that "poor folk" had to put up with this painful sort of life in poverty and crowded conditions.

Musically very gifted, he was first taught by the *regens chori* (choir master) of the parish church at Lichtenthal. Thanks to his voice and his talent he passed, at age 11, the tests required to become a student at the "Stadtkonvikt", and a choir boy in the Court Chapel. He was offered a place free of cost which gave the boy opportunities a child of poor parents could not otherwise have enjoyed. As choir boy he was really in the service of the Emperor and given free musical training by the most highly regarded teachers of the time, among whom was Salieri. Even his future was planned for. The students of the Stadtkonvikt were usually offered positions in the service of the Emperor if their parents did not have financial means to make other arrangements. The 11-year-old Schubert thus enjoyed the prospect of life-long security.

We know that he did not think much of security. He enjoyed the musical training and the friendships made at the Konvikt, he composed and made music, but he was not the kind of student who was anxious to "fit in." On the contrary, he often caused trouble and sympathized with the revolutionary movements then abroad.

His teachers recognized his talents. The school orchestra played his first little symphonies and he was given a special leave of absence to take lessons from Salieri—a demonstration of what we have mentioned several times, that musical talent was given every encouragement imaginable in Vienna. But Schubert did not stay at the Konvikt. His reasons for leaving the security of the institution were, on the one hand, an indomitable drive for freedom, as his teachers confirmed, and, on the other, the compulsion of "family circumstances." After Schubert's mother died, his father remarried and family circumstances changed, which led Schubert to the view that he had a responsibility to contribute to the upkeep of the family. He therefore left the Konvikt in 1813 and, after a training period of one and a half years, became an assistant teacher at his father's school. This experience led to great unhappiness, for he found teaching quite unrewarding and the salary was at best meager.

Only in his friendships with former fellow choir boys did he find any inspiration. Literature, music, social gatherings, part of his life at the Konvikt, were kept alive through

Of most of the great composers there are only a few portraits that can be called authentic. Very often they do not match the descriptions of contemporaries. Schubert's silhouette from the year 1817 may be fairly accurate.

these associations.

Much has been written about Franz Schubert, most of it after his early death. He is portrayed as very sociable; one who continued his childhood friendships all his life; and a particularly welcome member of social gatherings, called "Schubertiaden" (Schubert Evenings), in the homes of well-to-do citizens. But, as was adverted to only in passing at first but then more frequently: Schubert rarely demonstrated any interest in members of the opposite sex, though he composed love songs and played the piano while others danced. His sexual life seems to have been played out with prostitutes from one of whom he contracted syphillis in 1822. The number of musicians whose death can be traced to this disease, for which a cure was only recently developed, is amazingly high.

After three unhappy years of teaching, Schubert was given the welcome opportunity to resign and to live an independent life as a musician. His friend, Franz von Schober, undertook to provide him with money and living quarters. He also introduced the composer to the leading tenor in the Court Opera, Vogl, who made a place in history for himself by becoming Schubert's first successful interpreter and promoter.

Schubert subsequently spent two summers as a music tutor for the Esterházys at their estate in Hungary. While his letters to friends in Vienna reveal his yearning for city life, they can also reveal much about life at the castle. One letter reads like the idyllic setting for Eichendorff's *Aus dem Leben eines Taugenichts* (From the Diary of a Good-For-Nothing).

Other than the Esterházy sojourns Schubert scarcely left the city. He once visited Salzburg and was twice in Steyr. Save for three short trips he never ventured from the city whose citizens appreciated his music in his lifetime—contrary to the caricatures painted in operettas or popular stories. It is true that only a few of his symphonies were performed during his lifetime, but without question his songs, his chamber music, and his piano works were extremely popular with and frequently performed for the Vienna bourgeoisie, who were then on the rise and gradually assumed the role of a patron, formerly played by the nobility.

He did encounter great difficulty, however, in winning international recognition. Settings of Goethe's poems sent by Schubert's friends to His Excellency, the illustrious court poet, received only a polite confirmation of the receipt of the music, for Goethe, however great his gifts, was not well versed in music. The leading German music publishers accepted but few of Schubert's works for publication, though they were convinced of his talents and would probably have started to work with him had he lived longer. Only a few months before his death, he was advised that following the publication of a few of Beethoven's last works they would turn to Schubert. His social standing in Vienna, it must be admitted, was not particularly high. He was a free-lance musician associated with a young set, some of whom were purportedly involved in "revolutionary" circles—one even ended up in jail. He was at the center of an easy-going social circle, at times referred to as a drinking crowd. In short, he was not the sort of man whom respectable members of the bourgeoisie would have liked to have as a close friend or as a son-in-law. He was widely thought of as composer of dance music and waltzes, often mentioned in the same breath with Johann Strauss and Joseph Lanner, the entertainment musicians *par excellence.*

But he was also a board member of the Society of Friends of Music and as such well regarded by the "honorable" set of musicians. As a member of the governing body of this association he could have engineered, during the program planning sessions, performances of his works. He did not do so which is evident from the minutes. In this we discover one of his idiosyncrasies: He totally lacked any "wants" or "vanity." He seems to have been strangely uninterested in the fate or outcome of his productions. This same indifferent attitude can be gathered from statements of his contemporaries. But we have no documents in Schubert's hand in support of this idiosyncrasy, so must view it with some tenativeness.

Schubert was small and somewhat obese, wearing extremely thick glasses and thus not a very attractive looking man, and he seemed never to have any money. His friends and associates knew that he associated with prostitutes and drank to excess. Who could have called him the darling of the city? How could he be cast as the representative of Vienna's musical life? Until 1827, Schubert lived and worked in the "shadow of Beethoven," so how could he even hope to receive the accolades accorded that titan, who, since 1814, had an assured international position? From the conversation notebooks we know that Beethoven knew Schubert's compositions, played them on his piano, and made some very complimentary remarks about the composer.

We know of but a single personal meeting between the two musicians. A few days before Beethoven's death, Schubert, like other Viennese admirers, dared to visit the composer and was admitted at once. But until then Schubert, representing the music of the Vienna bourgeoisie, seems to have shied away from an interview with the favorite of the Viennese nobility. But this is only one interpretation of the facts, neither proven nor based on substantial documentation. That Schubert was convinced of his own capabilities as a musician and not afflicted by what was later called an inferiority complex is clear. His unique and personal approach to writing symphonies allows us to surmise that he felt sufficiently confident of his abilities, even at the height of Beethoven's fame, to pursue a different path.

When he wrote music like that of Beethoven or Johann Strauss the Elder,—an aspect of his work often overlooked—he was an inspired mediator between two quite

When Moritz von Schwind created this pen drawing in 1862, Franz Schubert—who died in 1828—was no longer merely a local celebrity, for even his more difficult works were widely performed. His former friend and recognized painter remembered in such drawings his own youth: Franz Lachner, Franz Schubert, and Eduard von Bauernfeld are sitting, in the evening, at a Heurigen in Grinzing.

distinct trends in Viennese music: Schubert's waltzes were published in volumes that also contained Strauss waltzes. Later generations admired and enjoyed Beethoven's and Schubert's German Dances and waltzes but failed to relate them to those of Strauss and Lanner. This discontinuity must clearly be laid at the feet of following generations, for in Schubert's time no music lover could have conceived of dividing music into the categories of "light" and "serious."

In 1826 the symptoms of Schubert's illness dating back to 1822 returned, and he suffered from frequent headaches and dizziness. But this year also witnessed a burst of creativity that lasted until the end and resulted in the creation of countless masterpieces. His great piano sonatas, his C Major Symphony, his song cycle *Die Winterreise* (Winter Journey) as well as the compilation of songs published after his death and titled by the publisher as the "cycle" *Schwanengesang* (Swan Song)—all date from this period.

In October 1828, he visited Haydn's grave, composed the song "Taubenpost" (Pigeon Mail), complained of attacks of vertigo, and refused to eat, asserting that someone had poisoned him. On 4 November he sought out the widely respected teacher of composition, Simon Sechter, for music instruction. He wished to study Bach and learn to write "real fugues, at long last." On 19 November he died at his brother's unfinished apart-

This drawing, also by Schwind, showing Schubert, Lachner, Schwind, and Vogl at a serenade, also has to be described as "drawn from memory". It could have inspired that unfortunate but popular operetta Das Dreimäderlhaus *(The Three Girls' Home). That is to say that even in 1862 Schubert was still seen in a romantic, sentimental haze.*

ment in a Vienna suburb, into which he had moved as a "dry-out tenant," a sobriquet given in those days to renters at a reduced rate of new buildings not yet ready for permanent occupation.

With such a brief account the outlines of Schubert's life can be summarized, for it was only after his death that the second and most astonishing phase of his existence began. Unlike the three composers dealt with earlier whose work was widely and warmly received in their lifetime and who were universally recognized as musical geniuses, Schubert was, after 1828, quickly forgotten. It was Robert Schumann, who, during his visits to Vienna, unearthed Schubert's "treasures" and sought to revive them, especially the symphonies. He was instrumental in having them performed in Germany and later in England. Quite surprisingly Schubert's symphonies remained virtually unplayed for decades and required many more years before they were accepted as a standard part of the concert repertoire, not as "fragments", but as coherent, complete pieces.

In fact one entire generation was required before Franz Schubert's work was seen as general property. Had it not been for friends who championed his songs and for the enthusiasm of numerous choral organizations who performed his many choral compositions, Schubert might have became an "idea" which simply disappeared.

Time worked slowly in favor of the composer. The interval, between the time when the Viennese bourgeoisie began to make music in their homes and when choirs adopted a large repertoire in which Schubert had a secure place, was long. Those who regarded Schubert as one of the "greats" of his time, judged wrongly. Wagner did not take him seriously. Brahms brought out a complete edition of his works only after all other important composers had been published in a similar manner. And the broad public did not know what to make of Schubert, other than identify him as the "Prince of Song." Indeed an operetta of that name unhappily styled him "Schwammerl" (mushroom), a reference to his puffy face.

In this connection it should be recalled that in his centenary year, 1928, a huge song festival was presented in Vienna, which was, above all, intended to serve as a propaganda tool aimed at the unification of Germany and Austria. At any rate, it was held in Schubert's honor, a century after his death, and though an abuse of his memory at least it fully recognized his important place in the pantheon of music.

The Time of the Minor Masters

The death of Franz Schubert marked the end of a glorious period in the history of the City of Music. For several following decades, no major composers lived permanently within its walls. The era following Schubert, though far from uninteresting or colorless, was one of "minor masters", an application given condescendingly to musicians whose compositions are not regularly a part of concert programs a generation or two after their deaths.

Perhaps we ought to remind ourselves that at Beethoven's graveside and, shortly thereafter, at that of Schubert's, aside from the Austrian poet and dramatist, Grillparzer, many of the same citizens and musicians gathered in homage. What were their names? They deserve mention here. They were solid and respected musicians at least some of whose works are still regularly performed in the city. But it is difficult in today's world to engender much interest in them or their compositions. There were, for example, two composers by the name of Müller, who are upon casual mention of their name frequently confused with each other, but both should be considered with some respect. They were Wenzel and Adolf Müller, no relation to each other, but kindred souls.

Wenzel Müller, born in 1759, hailed from Moravia, was a student of Karl Ditters von Dittersdorf and, from 1786 on, Kapellmeister at the Leopoldstädter Theater in Vienna. This is not quite correctly stated: The Leopoldstadt still was at that time one of the suburbs of Vienna within sight of the city center, situated toward the Danube. It was the suburb in which the Jewish population settled. The Leopoldstädter Theater, like its competitors in other suburbs beyond the city walls, had a loyal clientele which included those from the ranks of the Vienna bourgeoisie. It was a place where, like "On the Wieden", another suburban theater of Vienna, works by W. A. Mozart could be performed. Yet the real box office receipts came from popular presentations of magic tricks, farces, and plays depending upon scenery and scenery changes.

The "spectacles" staged took the place of those offered today by the movies and television, using remarkable technical devices capable of astonishingly fast scenery changes and other surprises. Their public was rarely required to follow complicated plots, but there was no end of entertainment and music appealing to the ear, music that was in no way trivial. The Kapellmeister at the various Viennese theatres could not afford to forget the audiences and their tastes when grinding out their music.

Wenzel Müller very successfully staged many plays of his own. He became the director of the Prague Opera House in 1807, but returned home after five years, and composed, in addition to his preceding successes, a *Travesty of the Magic Flute*, a play which he unashamedly hooked to the success of that of Mozart. He could in turn point out that many of his inventions had not been without public success. One of his songs, composed for the light opera *The Sisters from Prague*, was used by Beethoven for his Variations for Piano Trio, Op. 121. Wenzel Müller perhaps felt that his *Sisters from Prague* would never disappear entirely from the repertoire of the Vienna theaters, and it can still be heard occasionally. He died in 1835.

The other Müller, Adolf, called the Elder, hailed from Hungary, was born in 1801, and was, in his youth, not only a singer and actor, but soon also Kapellmeister. Today this title means merely director of the orchestra, but in those days it always also meant that he was the composer of many works performed by his ensemble. So Adolf Müller became

Kapellmeister when his first play was produced: first at the Theater at the Kärntnertor, the theater which later was to become the Court Opera House. But only a year later, in 1828,—the date of Schubert's death—he moved first to the Theater an der Wien and later in the same year to the Leopoldstädter Theater mentioned. "His operas, vaudevilles, parodies of local plays, and comedies dominated the repertoire of the Vienna stage for years," as the short entry in a music dictionary recounts. Such an entry is easy to write but does not convey anything of the untiring effort and richness of ideas of this Viennese resident theater composer, who not only produced and wrote his own plays, but also wrote the music for almost all of Johann Nestroy's many witty plays and—last but not least—managed to compose musical parodies of operas, mostly Italian, that were popular at that time, parodies that we find witty and entertaining even today. The catalogue of the works of Adolf Müller, who died in 1886, is endlessly long and his songs continue to be sung today, thanks to Nestroy's texts, or because they were once "hits" and Viennese singers have a very long memory! His complete plays no longer are familiar today but the proof of his genius as a stage musician lies in the fact that no better music has been written for Nestroy's plays to this day. And a knowledgeable public remains delighted when they hear that Müller's music is going to be played. It is useful to remind oneself that many a composer set Shakespeare's *Midsummer Night's Dream* to music but only Felix Mendelssohn-Bartholdy's is really known.

Conradin Kreutzer (1780–1849), known to music lovers for the title of his opera *Das Nachtlager zu Granada,* though the opera is no longer presented, was yet another of the minor composers of the time whom we must not forget. He too was not born in Vienna, but hailed from the German province of Baden. He travelled to the city to study with Johann Georg Albrechtsberger. The latter was Court Organist and Composer, and was generally remembered as the teacher of Beethoven and those minor masters like Johann Nepomuk Hummel, Ferdinand Ries, Joseph von Eybler, and Carl Czerny (the piano Czerny). Kreutzer, who was active in Vienna as composer and Kapellmeister until 1849, had thorough "serious" musical training writing both serious and lighter music. His career helps us understand why the lighter kind of "entertainment" music was not then so clearly distinguished from the "serious", classical kind as it is today. We do not wish to deal here with Kreutzer's serious music but rather turn to music that he wrote for Ferdinand Raimund's farce *Der Verschwender* (The Squanderer) which has proved enduring as any native Viennese will confirm. Some of the songs can be found under the heading "folk song" in modern German song books, a distinction which equals that given some melodies by Mozart or Schubert. Kreutzer's Viennese purlieus were the Kärntnertor Theater and the Josefstadt Theater, the theater in which Ferdinand Raimund's plays were produced. Kreutzer accepted, for a short time, an appointment abroad, but like his colleagues mentioned earlier, he "returned home," and all his great triumphs were celebrated in the city that he regarded as his second home. Franz Grillparzer, the great Austrian poet, whose great interest in music is seldom mentioned, was a close friend. Grillparzer had always hoped to write a libretto for Beethoven, but never did. But Grillparzer and Kreutzer collaborated on *Melusine,* an opera no longer performed.

Franz von Suppé, born later, (1819–1895), must not be overlooked in this brief account. A native of Split (Spalato) and a "cavaliere" (nobleman), he studied counterpoint and composition in Vienna, was called to the Theater an der Wien in 1845 and later (1863–1882) to the Carl Theater in the Leopoldstadt, a theater that was to become, later in the century, one of the leading stages for operetta in Vienna. Virtually all of his works are forgotten today, but their overtures are still found on the programs of the world's great orchestras. Whenever conductors are looking for a spirited and melodious overture they turn to those of Franz von Suppé. Their titles? *Poet and Peasant, Light Cavalry, Bandits' Tricks, Happy Fellows,* and *Fatinitza.* Moreover, two of his operettas are still occasionally presented in their entirety: *Boccaccio* and *Beautiful Galathea*. In calling attention to von Suppé's thorough music training I do so in order to close the arc from this composer of most entertaining Viennese music to two other musicians who stand, one at the beginning, the other at the end of the period of "minor masters", but who shared the same teacher.

Simon Sechter is a fascinating figure in Viennese music. Born in 1788 in Bohemia, Sechter studied in Vienna, became Court Organist in 1824 and had, by that time, developed a reputation as a first-rate teacher. He must have been a good one, as many music lovers suspect, for in every biography of Franz Schubert we learn that the composer enrolled as a student of counterpoint with Simon Sechter only a matter of weeks before his death. Many students of music history have attributed all kinds of fantastic motives to this. The critical question is: In what style had Schubert, the accomplished master, intended to compose when, in 1828, he suddenly decided to study strict counterpoint with a new teacher? What was his aim in doing so? What did Schubert think was lacking in the large volume of work that had been created without Sechter's assistance or instruction? What had he hoped to learn? All the answers offered to those questions are based on speculation and so are better forgotten.

It is a fact, however, that Simon Sechter, who was seriously sought after as a teacher by Schubert, from 1855 to 1861 did teach Anton Bruckner, and in such an intensive and thorough manner that soon after Sechter's death in 1867, Bruckner was appointed his successor, an appointment that surprised no-one. So, the arc extends from the great musician, Franz Schubert, to the great composer, Anton Bruckner, by way of this teacher of strict counterpoint. And from Bruckner it extends to Gustav Mahler, who may rightly be called Bruckner's student because he learned from the latter exactly that which Schubert, more than two generations before, had wanted to learn from Sechter.

Countless other students of Simon Sechter's also made their mark. Among them are highly respected and popular masters like Carl Zeller who, with his operetta *Der Vogelhändler* (The Bird Seller) has contributed to the standard German repertory. At any rate, after Antonio Salieri, whom we met earlier, Simon Sechter is a major figure in the continuous tradition of Viennese music: We should neither overemphasize continuity nor scoff at it. The fact is that there existed in Vienna, at the time when Arnold Schönberg lived there, a musical tradition that is readily traced and distinguishes that city—a tradition that reaches back to Gluck via Mahler, Bruckner, Sechter, Schubert and Salieri. If one considers how many other Viennese composers can similarly be traced back into the past, one is tempted to regard such musical ties not only as typical but as an advantage.

To turn to Schönberg once more—and we shall have to speak of him further in this book as the founder of a new school of musicians with its own tradition—as is well known Schönberg greatly admired Johannes Brahms' compositions and required his students to become thoroughly acquainted with them. Equally well known is how vigorously Brahms occupied himself with the work of Franz Schubert and how deeply interested he was in the works of Johann Sebastian Bach. While we cannot in each case point to a student-teacher relationship, I would like to remind my readers that musical episodes and events are linked in a complex web. Composers in all periods have looked back at the models of their predecessors with deep gratitude.

A city that can look back on a continuum of long-lived teachers who were also friends of the great musicians and can pass on a tradition—that is a City of Music.

And it is for this reason that Vienna is entitled to call itself just that. We need not have the names of the many composers who took up residence in the city for a short time only to make our point. That Carl Maria von Weber lived in Vienna seems natural. That Richard Wagner made it his home for a time should not be forgotten, but has never been taken very seriously either. That all those travelling musicians like Franz Liszt and Hector Berlioz took their sojourns in Vienna seriously can be easily comprehended. That Jacques

Offenbach celebrated his triumphs and that Johann Strauss Jr. wrote his operettas in Vienna is well understood. They together with many others enriched the musical life of this era that was an epoch between great epochs.

Johann Strauss Father and Sons

I have had occasion to mention this name earlier: the first Viennese King of Waltzes, the founder of a dynasty and *the* undisputed master of Viennese music. I have referred to his association with Schubert in one breath and mentioned his close link to contemporary classical composers. Johann Strauss the Elder put a lasting stamp on 19th-century Viennese music, and his son rounded it off.

Some might think I should write at length on the Viennese waltz at this point. To do so I would have to trace dance music in three-quarter time from the more sedate "Ländler" to the wild waltz rhythms, regarded at that time to be immoral by some. But what would such a recital tell us of the members of the Strauss dynasty? I could show that there had been musicians before them, known and anonymous, who had composed waltzes, and that a few waltzes can be found in the works of Mozart and others, but to what end? And to whom would it prove significant that at the beginning of the century there were composers of light music whose waltzes could have been heard by the two young violin players, Johann Strauss and Joseph Lanner? Suffice it here to recall that at the time the names of the elder Strauss and his friend and later rival, Lanner, became known to the public, the Viennese already knew and loved the waltz. But it was in the hands of those two that the Viennese waltz found its place as the great musical event of the century. We can confidently equate the first Viennese Waltz Kings with Mozart, Schubert or Bruckner, and have no qualms about so doing. Strauss in particular truly earned his position as the sire of a whole dynasty as he had so thoroughly mastered the qualities and skills necessary to the Viennese waltz composer *"par excellence"* and was to be the model for his sons.

Johann Baptist Strauss was born in 1804 in Vienna. His Jewish ancestry led to a quite remarkable incident at the time of Adolf Hitler. In a quite fantastic and unbelievable sequence of events, it was "proved" that Strauss was not Jewish so that Strauss waltzes could be played without any qualms in a purely "Aryan" society. He took some violin lessons, and studied music theory, and joined a small orchestra of entertainment musicians headed by Michael Pamer (whose compositions are still heard today) as a viola player. In 1819 he joined up with Joseph Lanner, another Viennese musician, born in 1801. They first formed a quartet, then a somewhat larger orchestra, playing at their own risk and expense in Vienna restaurants. Relying on the great musical interest of the public, one of the members of the orchestra circulated among the tables from time to time to gather contributions. This practice was common at that time and brought in enough income to sustain the players. As is probably clear to my readers, musicians such as Strauss and Lanner were not considered as belonging to the best social classes.

The repertory of such orchestras included waltzes. Of course, they were not waltzes as we know them today or think of them today. The waltz was not a Viennese invention, but was used for dance music around 1750 in rural areas of Salzburg and Upper Austria along the Danube River. It finally reached Vienna after being mixed with other dance music forms, particularly the "Deutsche." The latter was a German dance viewed at that time as rather crude, even erotic.

In its early form—and a point we must not forget—it was repeatedly forbidden, because couples did not just join hands gracefully and decently, but crudely placed their

In the valuable collection called Vienna Folk Songs of Five Centuries *this portrait of Joseph Lanner is included among all sorts of curios. He was at first the associate, later the competitor of Johann Strauss, the Elder. It was decades before the more retiring of the great composers of waltzes was appreciated again. Johann Strauss, Junior had swept aside all other composers.*

arms around each other, and rather than walking daintily side by side, whirled around each other until they often fell from dizziness, a desired finale to the dance. Such carryings-on were seen as thoroughly vulgar and crude, but the inhabitants of the city, in imitation of their country cousins, adopted them with outward expression of disgust but simultaneously with great enthusiasm, and at last made the waltz their own.

The musicians who composed waltzes before Strauss and Lanner took their principal inspiration from bands that called themselves "Linzer Geiger" (Violinists from Linz)—bands that had moved down the Danube from Linz to play that kind of dance music in Vienna. The earliest waltz musicians are largely unknown today, with one notable exception. The Vienna music publisher, Anton Diabelli, wrote down a waltz theme and sent it to all composers known to him, asking them to write variations on the theme. The responses are known today by the name of the *Diabelli Variations.* There are in fact two very different versions of these variations. One is the series which resulted from the many replies to his request, written by a number of composers. The other is the series written by Ludwig van Beethoven alone, and known as Op. 120, the last really great piano work of the Titan.

The second generation of Viennese waltz composers is not well documented, but when in 1819 Carl Maria von Weber wrote his *Invitation to the Dance* laying the foundation for the form of the concert waltz with symphonic introduction followed by several waltzes and ending with a coda that rounded off the piece, Strauss and Lanner were not yet composing waltzes but only playing those of others. At any rate, they played together for some years, then had a falling out and thereafter competed with one another. This competition forced them to seek out new and different compositions, and hardly ever has there been a more fruitful competition with more enjoyable results, for each started composing waltzes for his orchestra. Johann Strauss began with his "Täuberl Waltz (Little Dove Waltz) of 1826, and wrote before his death 250 compositions, more than 150 of them waltzes.

Let me interrupt here momentarily, for a "correction" seems to be in order: To be really correct we should always refer to Viennese "waltzes" in the plural form, for they are really a set of several independent little waltzes, which could not, under any circumstances, have a larger form or shape. Just how they are connected or harmonize with one another is a distinctive feature of such a set. The first waltz usually justifies the title given to the whole set and provides a handle for the whole chain of waltzes.

As we know from an advertisement that appeared in the official Vienna newspaper, Johann Strauss published waltzes in a thin volume in which some of Schubert's were also printed. This publication proves that the form had been recognized and established as such. Schubert and Beethoven wrote waltzes either as such, or as passages in 3/4 time incorporated into their works which one could call in good faith "secret" waltzes. There never seemed to have been a question of drawing a line between entertainment and serious music at that time, just as no distinction was made between creative musicians and interpreters. Every musician could make music on his instrument or as a singer, and all were able to produce something original, limited only by the talent of each. It was unthinkable that a musician was "just" a violinist, devoting his life exclusively to the interpretation of works written by others.

What placed Johann Strauss, and for the sake of orderliness we must give him his correct name, Johann Strauss the Elder, over and above the others was his wealth of musical ideas, his personality as a violinist and his rarely appreciated commercial acumen in exploiting his talents. He became much more than just another Kapellmeister of a popular entertainment orchestra in Vienna. He organized countless festivities for which admission fees were charged. He sought out other musicians in order to use compositions, if they were successful, in his own performances. He took advantage of every social or public event of any size to dedicate to it one of his own compositions. He was careful to

Johann Strauss

Joseph Strauss

have printed music ready for sale, so the music-loving public might be able to play every successful piece again at home. This careful and minute attention to commercial exploitation spread the fame and lure of the name Johann Strauss.

All members of the dynasty, beginning with Strauss the Elder, had, moreover, an exotic element both in their behavior and appearance. All had dark complexions, black hair, were rather excitable,—they never gave the impression of being sedate Viennese, but rather appeared foreign. These qualities are easily forgotten when reflecting today upon the members of the Strauss family as typical native Viennese. Much about them was almost gypsy-like and anything but typical. And it was just those qualities which led the Viennese to adore these violinists and conductors who thrashed the air with their arms and violin bows.

It can safely be said that Johann Strauss the Elder employed every means at his disposal to promote his image. And so he saw it as a matter of course that he and his orchestra travel endlessly, from one princely court to another and to any social gathering of any importance. These excursions were invariably reported in dispatches offering glowing reports of his successes to the press at home.

None of this would ever have led to the title "King of the Waltz" and all the glory that went with it, if Johann Strauss had not written such a tremendous quantity of really inspired music and had not played it fairly well. Nor should we forget that although we always think of all members of the dynasty with violins in their hands, we must not imagine them as bewitching virtuosos on that instrument. Any competent violinist of the time possessed as much if not more technical skill than Johann Strauss was able to offer, but none of them possessed such a demoniacal obsession for public acclaim as he.

The works of Strauss the Elder are readily distinguished from those of his sons, because those of the former have an agreeable, solid bourgeois quality and because they do not display truly intoxicating inspiration. Today we might rather call them endearing, alluring. And yet they were considered fiery in their time and had all the qualities that make today's entertainment music attractive to us: the rhythm, the presence, the quick, hot-blooded Viennese "impudence", the readily remembered, catchy melodies.

In 1833 Strauss the Elder's orchestra, consisting of 28 men, began touring. In 1834

These silhouettes of the brothers Strauss were as popular in Vienna as the conducting and fiddling Kapellmeister themselves. Johann Strauss, the Waltz King, Joseph Strauss, his silent brother, and Eduard Strauss, known as "handsome Ed," when he toured the world with his orchestra.

Eduard Strauss

47

he became Kapellmeister of the First Vienna Citizens' Regiment, and in 1835 he was finally made director of the Viennese Court Dance Orchestra. The Court appointment obliged him, with only a small stipend as a reward, to provide and improve the musical offerings of the Court Balls. He was able to make up for the modest income by becoming known elsewhere, by virtue of his title and reputation. No doubt he made the most of this situation, and he had a faithful publisher.

With his devoted though not adoring wife he had three sons, who grew, much against his will, into an entire dynasty. For some time after his death little was publicly said of his family life, and little was quoted from remarks and newspaper advertisements in which Strauss, Jr. speaks of his relation to his father. But it is hard to keep secrets forever: today we know that Johann Strauss, who was either on tour or fully occupied in Vienna, racing from one dance engagement to another, was followed, as all good artists are, by a whole flock of female admirers, making it easy to depart from the role of a solid *"pater familias"* and devoted family man. He was soon estranged from his family. Though officially still married, he lived with a mistress whose name was Trampusch, and of whom it was said that she was a vulgar, ordinary, unkempt woman. However, she must have exercised a certain attraction for the always overtired musician and offered him and the several children she bore him a substitute for the family life he had deserted, or he would not have stayed with her for so many years.

The responsibility for his legitimate sons rested with Anna Strauss, a woman to whom musical history has paid too little attention. It was she who encouraged Johann Strauss, Jr. to study music and to obtain instruction in violin playing fairly early in life, against the will of his father. And it was she who convinced the boy to join the family enterprise, after Strauss the Elder's death, as a violinist and ultimately Kapellmeister and composer. It was she who bore the entire responsibility for allowing the sons to become musicians, against the express wish of their father.

Johann Strauss Jr., born in 1825, soon after the separation of his parents began the study of composition with the highly respected Joseph Drechsler, composer of music for the Raimund plays. He founded his first orchestra in 1844 and performed in competition with his father during the latter's lifetime. Joseph Strauss, born in 1827, might have become an engineer, had he been left to his own devices. But he often had to substitute for his elder brother in conducting the Strauss Jr. orchestra and was soon caught up in the family business. Eduard Strauss, born in 1835, was brought up entirely by his mother, for his father left the family at this time. He studied composition and soon provided at first modest, but thereafter ever more important services to his two brothers. He outlived both, dying in 1916. He was, no doubt, a significant member of the family but was the son who did not achieve the same fame as a composer. When he decided to dissolve his orchestra and give no more public concerts he rented a Vienna studio with a large pipe stove and supervised the incineration of all the sheet music used by his orchestra. Though this behavior was completely irrational, he wanted, so to speak, to destroy the characteristic sound on which his success had been based. He left some "Memoirs" which are only of use to those who know enough of the family history to recognize those events the aging Eduard intended to present in a more favorable light.

But to return to Johann Strauss the Elder and the family chronicle. Let us acknowledge that, though he was no longer a family man, he was the undisputed sovereign of Viennese entertainment music and a faithful subject to his Emperor. During this period, now called "Vormärz" (the time before the Revolution in March 1848, and one of oppression and poverty), his music was thoroughly beloved by the public and tolerated by the authorities, a combination rarely encountered at that time. Strauss's music was not regarded as revolutionary, but rather as benevolent, an escape from the troubles of the time, a rare combination of good taste and political expediency. Partly because of this, one could not imagine in 1848 that the competition between father and son would eventually end in the son's favor. The stories of the tensions between father and son were repeatedly turned into operettas and novels, but are now very difficult to prove. Strauss Jr. must have found it very painful to grow up without a father and to see his mother suffer. The Viennese public was fascinated by the fact that he had taken up music against his father's wishes, but more fascinating today is to *hear* how Strauss Jr. gradually broke away from the model of his father's waltzes, and how long it took him to learn to write music as popular as that of his parental competitor who even near the very end created such a success as the "Radetzky March."

When, in 1848, revolution broke out in Vienna Strauss the Elder demonstrated his loyalty by remaining quietly and undemonstratively in the background. His son, on the other hand, played the role of the rebellious young man for some time and even in the spirit of the times performed the Marseillaise, the hymn of the French Revolution. But when, by the end of the year, Emperor Francis Joseph I had taken over the government and had eliminated all resistance, Strauss Jr. recognized that he had gambled on the wrong party. Wrong, above all, for a musician who was counting on support from higher circles, on impressive titles and rewards. Years later the Imperial Court still remembered that young Strauss had not been as loyal as his father. Only his obvious success as composer of waltzes made it possible for him to be recognized, first by the public at large, but then also by the aristocracy as the new King of the Waltz and eventually as the only Strauss worthy of the title.

When Strauss the Elder died in 1849, at the abode of his mistress, Strauss Jr. sought to restore the reputation of the family. He published the famous announcement requesting the favor of his father's former patrons. In truth it was his mother, who at long last and for many years thereafter benefited and who took charge of the dynasty's affairs.

Anna Strauss negotiated contracts; looked after family matters; and managed the musical affairs of the Strauss orchestras, of which there were several, so that the composer often had to appear in several places in a single evening. She persuaded brother

Johann Strauss Junior was no longer a native of the Leopoldstadt (the Jewish quarter of Vienna), but of the Lerchenfelderstrasse, in the outskirts. His close ties to his Jewish ancestors, who were mostly residents of the Leopoldstadt, are no longer evident. These ties were also erased from the records during the time of National Socialism.

Joseph to give up his profession and become a musician like the others—a decision that may not have been all to the good. Joseph Strauss, a few of whose waltzes became very famous but whom many an expert thought superior to his brother, suffered ill-health throughout his life. The obligations placed upon him led to living a very public life involving much night work and extensive travel, both at home and abroad. This arduous schedule ruined his health and he died in 1870, very much earlier than he might have as a civil engineer. But we must be grateful to the domineering Anna Strauss and her determination to turn all her sons into musicians, for this resulted in many unforgettable Joseph Strauss waltzes. It is difficult to reproach an ambitious mother. Time has certainly proved that she pursued a wise course.

And yet Johann Strauss Jr. might not have reached such heights of fame during his lifetime, both in Vienna and abroad, had good fortune not placed in his way a few very special engagements and a handful of very special musical acquaintances. From Imperial Russia came a timely invitation to play promenade concerts for an entire summer at the terminal of a newly built railroad. By accepting the invitation he became a musical hero far from home. The important and rich citizens of St. Petersburg who used this railroad showered him with money and fame upon his departure.

It was this single success abroad, but then repeated many summers, that gained him the esteem of the Viennese. His custom of playing at his Vienna concerts not only the latest of his own compositions but also those of his contemporaries, as well as concert versions of popular operas, earned the approval and gratitude of important composers throughout Europe. They returned the favor by extolling the musical qualities of their Viennese protagonist in their own countries. Richard Wagner, for example, whose music was still regarded as revolutionary, was played regularly by Strauss, leading him to become an admirer. Hector Berlioz, who had been a friend of Strauss the Elder and a financial backer of Strauss concerts in Paris, was quite opposed to Wagner yet he, too, became an enthusiastic supporter of young Strauss's music. Johannes Brahms was, when he finally moved to Vienna, often a guest at the Strauss home and never failed to demonstrate his friendship and admiration for the musicianship of Johann Strauss. We could continue with this enumeration of composers who, though they did not agree with one another, did agree, "nolens volens", on their regard for Johann Strauss waltzes. More than 300 compositions, among them the most popular of all Strauss waltzes, had been composed when Johann Jr. was persuaded to write an operetta. His wife's ambitions and the success Jacques Offenbach enjoyed in Vienna were, in the general opinion, the mainspring for his entry into the new theatrical field. Strauss's critics contended from the outset that all of his operettas were really only an extension of his dance and waltz sequences, and would only be considered successful if a goodly number of great waltzes could be extracted from them. There is more than a kernel of truth in this criticism: Whatever shortcomings modern music criticism finds in the genre "operetta" occurs in pure form in most of Strauss' works. The strange, if not completely illogical twists in the story line; the crude or indeed cruel treatment of language; the absurd obsession with creating situations in which well known comedians or a dance troupe could be used—all were used by Strauss but proved beyond doubt that his wonderful music could bolster up the silliest of operettas. His public was always attracted to and satisfied with a few main numbers, rather than the work as a whole.

It is contended today that *Die Fledermaus* (The Bat) and *Der Zigeunerbaron* (The Gypsy Baron) are laudable exceptions. But this is quite unfair to his other operettas. If analyzed in detail, one is forced to agree with Karl Kraus that these two works are typical of his operettas, i.e., superficially worked out stage plays. These two are, however, studded with superb melodies, while melodic jewels are more sparsely scattered in all the others. Therein lies all the difference.

The great success of Jacques Offenbach inspired Johann Strauss to compose operettas. When his "Die Fledermaus" (The Bat) had become really serious competition, the humorous magazine "New Free Cock-a-Doodledo" (a somewhat clumsy allusion to the respected "New Free Press") published this caricature, called "On Olympus," in 1874.

The relative unimportance of the libretto is clearly evident in his *Eine Nacht in Venedig* (A Night in Venice), for example. It was a total failure in Berlin, but then had a respectable success at the Vienna premiere, probably a patriotic response to the poor Berlin reception. Many years later after innumerable revisors had had a go at the story, enriching themselves thereby, the music of Johann Strauss, in the end, still always guaranteed the approval of the audience, irrespective of what was happening on the stage.

The list of works by Johann Strauss Jr. numbers 479. Most of them were given a title of their own soon after their composition, or their first performance, and the fact that all were either dedicated to or performed at special occasions or for particular organizations or well-known persons helped the public remember them and extol their virtues. Strauss the Elder, who found his place in music history not only as a composer, but as a master of self advertisement as well, had in his son not simply a successor but one who outdid him in promotional skills. Not only in his methods of winning public support and his mastery of selling his music, but also in his ability to derive profit from his mere presence at a concert, Johann Strauss was a genius in his time. All the tricks employed by today's commercialized pop music producers, including extensive publicity campaigns to promote a new record or pop group, are but variations on themes developed by Strauss Jr. But today's practitioners fall far short of the Strauss success. Lacking all the technology of modern communication and transportation, without radio, without television, without records, without jet aircraft, Johann Strauss Jr. managed to become a matinée idol around the world and to eclipse the fame of local celebrities: composers of waltzes in Paris, entertainment musicians in Berlin, Gilbert and Sullivan in the Anglo-American world.

He was never refused the recognition he so avidly sought. He held an assured and unparalleled position of respect in the Austro-Hungarian Monarchy, witness: he resigned his post as Court Ball Music Director when *he* chose to do so and yet was able to demand the medal due to him from his Emperor. His application for this decoration still exists; in it

Johann Strauss Jr. summarized all the things which he had done for Vienna and the Imperial House, and despite the required submissive tone we can still sense in every sentence the self-esteem of the musician who could call himself King of the Waltz in the Imperial City.

His death in 1899 shocked the world. His funeral was a last triumphal procession through Vienna. A good portion of his estate was made over to the Society of Friends of Music in whose archives many of his manuscripts are still safely stored. His fame was not to come decades after his death, rather it was his when he died and it lasted for generations, to this very day. Moreover it is not confined to the dancing public, but all musicians after him who carried this art further revered the man. Even Arnold Schönberg and his school ungrudgingly recognized the genius of Johann Strauss Jr. Present-day composers when given the opportunity imitate Strauss: when asked to compose a waltz they honor him by doing so, as was recently exemplified by Luciano Berio, or they translate one of his compositions into their own orchestral idiom, as Dimitri Shostakovich has done on several occasions.

Johannes Brahms

It's strange, but Johannes Brahms, hailing from Hamburg, was never regarded as a real Viennese, though he lived in Vienna for many years, received many honors and in the end was accepted by the Viennese as a composer of their city. The case is quite different with Beethoven, whose origin in Bonn on the Rhine is seldom recalled today and who is indeed regarded as an integral part of Viennese Classicism. The native of Hamburg, Brahms, is to this day regarded as a typical North German and much is still told of him that seems foreign or alien. While many biographies and learned papers have been written about him and his work, there is some evidence that he has not yet been "discovered."

Brahms was born on May 7, 1833. His father was a professional musician, one of the more modest kind, playing the contrabass in light music ensembles, at first not even in the most fashionable places of entertainment. Johannes Brahms' mother was 17 years older than her husband and must have had a strong character. Brahms was brought up like a kind of minor prodigy. He received piano lessons at an early age and soon appeared in public, but was not, as had been the fashion, handed round and exhibited, but performed only in his father's circles: this is to say he played the piano in ensembles whenever his father had to perform for dances. We know that he played practically always by heart and mechanically, for instead of music scores he had books on the piano rack in front of him. Due to family circumstances he was not able to complete his higher education but studied whenever he was able to.

The Vienna music critic Max Graf, well remembered for his championing of Anton Bruckner before the turn of the century, tells in one of his books of an evening when he encountered Johannes Brahms in a Viennese restaurant that was all but elegant. The composer had been asked to play dance music for a somewhat inebriated party, so for hours he played old-fashioned tunes on an old, out-of-tune piano—reminiscing all the while of his earlier days when he earned his living in this way.

Brahms' first piano teacher recommended him to Eduard Marxen, then known in Hamburg as an outstanding composer, and it was he who was responsible for the solid musical foundation that Brahms had acquired by the time he began to go on tour. At the age of 20, as a competent pianist but as yet a completely unknown composer who had no works published and nothing ready to show, he accompanied a Hungarian violinist on his first concert tour. The two young musicians traveled through Germany in a carefree, casual manner, often on foot and never in a position to appear as triumphant virtuosos, yet curious and ready for adventure.

Brahms was received by Franz Liszt in Weimar and promptly spoiled his first opportunity. He was a good-looking young man with a high voice and boyish manner and might have had an opportunity to start a career in the circle of the famous Liszt, had he but been polite. But he did not hesitate to make known his dislike of the virtuoso's music, adding that it meant nothing to him. He was too honest.

However, he had another opportunity which he seized upon. Joseph Joachim, at that time far from having a world-wide reputation as a violinist, recommended Brahms to Clara and Robert Schumann. Although Brahms was not enthusiastic about Schumann's music, he managed to impress the composer, and after playing for them he developed an immediate and close tie to the couple. Schumann wrote an enthusiastic article, entitled

"New Ways" (Neue Bahnen) in the music magazine he had founded but no longer edited, announcing that he thought that although he had completed only a few compositions Brahms was the genius Germany had been waiting for, ever since the deaths of Beethoven and Schubert. At about the same time he interested a publisher in Brahms and did everything that a young musician could hope for in his wildest dreams. We still do not know today just what the purely human relationships between Brahms and Clara and Robert really were.

But let us proceed to the Vienna composer Brahms. Half a year after this first meeting, Schumann, who had been ill for quite some time, tried to commit suicide and was put into an asylum. He no longer had regular contact with his wife, but through occasional letters and personal visits, remained in touch with his young protege, Brahms. Schumann remained in this institution until his death, sending strange notes to Brahms who, as a close friend of the family, was staying with Clara Schumann. He undertook the strange role of "go-between", but also at long last began seriously to compose. After Schumann's death Brahms concentrated on his own career and gradually became famous far and wide as a composer and pianist, though having some difficulty in freeing himself from Clara Schumann's influence. He soon thereafter became the standard bearer of a group of musicians who refused to join the circle around Liszt. His obvious objective, though he never admitted it openly, was to obtain a distinguished position in his native city. Countless references in his letters make it clear that he would have welcomed an appointment in his native city at any time. But while failing to realize his goal in Hamburg he did just this in Vienna, where his pilgrimage had taken him like so many other musicians before him.

From 1862 onward Brahms can be spoken of as one who lived and worked in Vienna, found friends and followers, was engaged as the conductor of the *Singakademie* (Choral Society); and later became the director of the *Singverein* of the Society of

The slim, dreamy looking youth, Johannes Brahms, who appeared to Schumann to be the incarnation of true genius that he had long hoped for, became in his advancing years, at least in his exterior appearance, a rather stout, rather pedestrian looking "Viennese pope of music." Willy von Beckerath made these drawings of the conducting composer "from life" in Frankfurt in 1895.

Friends of Music. He was welcomed with deep appreciation, and was never given any cause to leave thereafter. He repeatedly tried to obtain an appointment in Germany commensurate with his success and was, at times, active elsewhere but always returned to Vienna. He had his Vienna apartment and adopted the Viennese style of living; he had a large circle of friends in Vienna, but his beloved library still remained in Hamburg. The composer Brahms, who only after much hesitation and delay began his first symphony, consciously following the footsteps of Beethoven, was known all over the world, and his choral works, piano pieces and chamber music had brought him financial success. He was a person of distinction, visible to all the world as a resident of Vienna. Until his death he was, according to all accounts, a learned, wise, benign, but also grumpy man, the friend of musicians and an "independent bachelor," as he liked to call himself. All his life he shied away from close ties to women, remaining to his death a typical North German bachelor in Vienna. Even today no one has been able to explain the conflict between his outer and his inner personality, the gap between the gradually aging "elderly gentleman" and the youthful fire and passion of his music. As Brahms was a master of all musical forms including the most complex ones, he could be regarded as a successor of both Bach and Beethoven, and one might even forget that he was in reality a true Romantic. Although he repeatedly made it known that he desired a serious relationship with a woman, no one could really conceive of linking him to any other passions. A rumor without verification had it that he was the perfect example of a secret homosexual, and at one time or another an attempt surely will be made to document this theory.

When he did not opt for solitude, Brahms, as is well known, enjoyed pleasant social contacts in Vienna. Brahms and Johann Strauss Jr. admired each other, as evidenced musically speaking in the *Liebesliederwalzer* (Love Song Waltzes) by Brahms which are deeply felt expressions of his admiration for the waltz. Further documentation is found in the famous phrase penned beneath the first measures of the *Blue Danube Waltz:* "Unfortunately not by your Johannes Brahms."

The very close relationship with the Viennese music critic and theoretician, Eduard Hanslick, is evident in the correspondence between the two as well as in Hanslick's Memoirs. This relationship had as one of its key elements the fact that both Hanslick and Brahms were recognized throughout Europe as the explicit opponents of Richard Wagner and his musical ideas. Unfortunately this opposition is greatly oversimplified today. Hanslick was not a malicious adversary of Wagner, but rather a consistent critic of aesthetic principles. Brahms suffered, no doubt, from the fact that, following his first unfortunate meeting with Liszt, he was aligned with the circle of "Young Germany" musicians—anathema to the Wagnerians. What Wagner himself really thought of Brahms has not to date been discovered. General opinion without any clear evidence has it that Wagner hated his rival. But reading Cosima Wagner's diary leads to the conclusion that Wagner saw Brahms as a serious competitor. Wagner concerned himself too seriously with Johannes Brahms' music to have truly despised him.

Dr. Theodor Billroth, a Viennese surgeon of considerable renown, also a bachelor and lover of music, was a close associate of Brahms and Hanslick.

And finally we must take note of the high society of Vienna in which Brahms consistently moved despite his deliberate rudeness but always pleased to receive recognition. Let no one forget that Brahms, like "tout Vienne", spent his summers in Bad Ischl, in Upper Austria, the Imperial summer residence and watering hole of the "haut monde." Nor that he carried sufficient weight with the music publishers that he was able to assist gifted young composers like Antonin Dvorak in having their work reach a wider public. He was at home in all those Viennese circles from which Anton Bruckner, who was no longer young, felt himself excluded. Both bachelors, Brahms and Bruckner had their reserved tables, shared with their "cronies," in very modest Viennese restaurants. Under different circumstances they might have established a fairly close friendship. As it was, they were at home in two different social strata which were mutually exclusive. It was Brahms who was gladly received by well established society.

Music lovers at that time report that Johannes Brahms, despite serious illness, not only attended the requiem mass for Anton Bruckner held at the Vienna St. Charles Church, but also that he cried. It is possible that the differences in station stood in the way of a social relationship, but the musician Brahms did not completely reject the musician Bruckner, a legend initiated in eagerly read critical articles by Eduard Hanslick, who had taken his stand against Bruckner.

Numerous anecdotes of that time turn on a world-famous composer who was a "loner;" was occasionally invited to dinner or to a bachelor party where he was relatively at ease; had a faithful housekeeper; and lived contentedly, after receiving his library from Hamburg, in a house next to the Karlskirche. He was an enthusiastic collector of musicians' autographs, and characterized himself in numerous letters to friends and other musicians as shy and taciturn. He was sufficiently well-to-do that he could help impecunious fellow musicians or friends, something he did often, generously and tactfully. Lastly he never gave up his contacts with relatives in Hamburg and in an anxious and touching manner endeavored to remain on familiar terms with them long after he had really lost all intimate contact with them.

Vienna is indebted to the musician Brahms not only for his compositions but also his informed appreciation of the Viennese life style, and more importantly as the author of the Schubert renaissance. Brahms was not only an avid collector of Schubert autographs, but also devoted much time and energy to seeing the first complete edition of Schubert's works into print. Well-known conductors are commonly credited as the first performers of Schubert's symphonies, decades after his death, yet Brahms' role is unfortunately overlooked and due praise does not accrue to him. Not only did he play many of Schubert's

The Society of Friends of Music in Vienna, principal heir to Brahms' estate, owns, among other treasures, this silhouette by Otto Böhler, showing Brahms on his way to the "Red Hedgehog," his favorite tavern.

works in his recitals, but unfailingly promoted Schubert's music in every forum in which he had a voice, pointing to the richness of the treasure still to be discovered.

In this he was the legitimate successor to his beloved Robert Schumann who during his short visits to Vienna never ceased to be amazed at Schubert's music and who repeatedly drew attention to Schubert in his *Zeitschrift* as long as he was its editor.

When Johannes Brahms died on April 3, 1897 Vienna understood that one of the world's most important composers was forever gone. The city paid its homage by staging one of its "pomp and circumstance" funerals. Brahms left most of his earthly goods to the Society of Friends of Music in Vienna; they are proud that their archives hold the composer's manuscripts and autographs, as well as his beloved library.

Johannes Brahms expressly wrote for the large concert hall of the Society with the consequence that his works were conceived for orchestras and halls that still exist today. When attending performances of any of his forerunners we hear them, so to speak in translation from another time. But this is not the case with Brahms, who was one of the foremost creators of bourgeois music culture which remains alive and well in Vienna to this day.

We tend to see Brahms as the conservative counterplayer to 19th-century progress in music and so side, for instance, with the vehement attacks that the young Hugo Wolf, a student of Bruckner, launched against Brahms. We are still ready to see in Brahms only the protagonist of conservative young musicians like Antonin Dvorak. But this is a one-sided view and therefore unfair. Arnold Schönberg not only respected Brahms as a master of musical form, but also had reason to be personally grateful to him. Hanns Eisler, a student of Schönberg's, expressly notes that his teacher's first compositions had drawn Brahms' attention, and also that Richard Strauss had in correspondence commented on Brahms' insight when considering new compositions submitted to him. In short, we do Brahms an injustice if we see in him a man who only looked back. He looked to the future as well, and understood that the future was going to be musically exciting. When advising young composers to study strict and really old-fashioned "theory" thoroughly he did nothing else than did Schönberg, one of the avowed innovators a little later. Schönberg, too, was not only a revolutionary, but a master of strict counterpoint.

Anton Bruckner

The name of the "other" important Viennese composer of Brahms' time has appeared several times here. Anton Bruckner, to this day thought of (at least in Austria) as Brahms' opposite, actually is simply "another" composer of the time. He should not be judged in such a way—an easy cliché which has been handed down from one generation of Viennese to another. Nor can the image of the naïve, rural "musician of God," hopelessly lost in the abysmally sinful metropolis, Vienna, an image attributable to his modest and benign bearing, be supported. This caricature had been repeated over and over again, both in the popular press and in learned theses. But the recent Bruckner jubilee year and the growing body of information on his life and work has destroyed this image once and for all.

There is nothing new about this. Unsupportable legends about musicians of other generations also circulated widely until debunked by scholarship. All too often musicians are regarded as some strange species of saint, so little notice is taken of their human characteristics and consequent conflicts with the mores of their times. The child prodigy "Wolferl" (nickname for Wolfgang) Mozart, "God's organ player" (Bruckner), the unreciprocated lover "Schwammerl" (Schubert), and the "Titan" (Beethoven), were never living figures but icons created, and admired by music lovers.

Anton Bruckner's beginnings were much like those of other great musicians. He was born on September 4, 1824 in Ansfelden in Upper Austria. There was musical talent on his father's and grandfather's side. Trained in basic musical skills, he was able to substitute for his father as a church organist at the age of 10. Like Brahms he learned the practical side at an early age, but in his case in the church, not the dance hall. Yet we can assume that in such rural surroundings he was also exposed to the more worldly uses of music.

Bruckner became a boy chorister at the Monastery of St. Florian—not the first choir boy to become world famous. His life continued under the guardianship of his clerical protectors, for when he left he became the school assistant in several small villages in the vicinity of the monastery. He eventually became a virtuoso on the organ so that at the age of 21 he was appointed organist of the Cathedral at Linz, the capital of Upper Austria.

Aware that he could not acquire more than average training in musical theory in Linz, he travelled to Vienna to become a student of Simon Sechter, a well-known and strict teacher. He soon landed his first appointment as "Instructor of Music" for future teachers of music at the Teachers' Training College, for at the time music was an important, required subject in the training of teachers. He continued to study and to play the organ, but also began to compose. He finished his first symphony long before he was 25. Later, in the catalogue of his works, it came to be counted as "Symphony No. Zero."

In 1868, succeeding his own teacher, he became a Professor of Harmony, Counterpoint and Organ at the Vienna Conservatory, then the only such institution in the Imperial capital. Now let us stop to think for a moment: Here we have a young musician of whom it will later be said that all his life he had to endure constant degradation, derision, and setbacks. This brief biography leads to a different conclusion. Here in fact is a peasant's son from Upper Austria who is now Professor of Harmony and Counterpoint in one of the world's capitals of music, who is acquiring a worldwide reputation as an organist; who is invited to play the organ at Nancy and Paris in France, and at the Royal

Albert Hall in London, where he is fêted as a sensational virtuoso. He was only 40 by then, and therefore had no reason to bow or defer to other musicians or shyly or helplessly stand aside.

However, there still are a few music experts who tell other stories of Bruckner. For example that he acted the peasant before his students at moments when he deemed it right to do so, or would unashamedly act the adoring admirer of his musical idols. Yet he was conscious of his own position and, in private moments, did not hesitate to tell others that he counted himself as an equal to those of whom he usually spoke modestly and admiringly. His students vouched for this and oral tradition confirms it.

Self-esteem aside, Bruckner, the devout organist and symphonist, had but one idol: Richard Wagner. Bruckner came to know and admire the genius of Bayreuth and gratefully accepted the latter's condescending but friendly words. The announcement of Wagner's death saddened Bruckner as no other event before or after. There were undoubtedly several reasons behind this admiration of Wagner, including at least one outside the field of music. Bruckner, educated by the Church and full of Christian humility, must have been attracted and impressed by the pomp and circumstance of Wagner's stage settings and by the general atmosphere of his works. Bruckner most likely understood that Wagner deliberately placed himself beyond and above all accepted rules and could therefore not be compared to anyone else.

Moreover, Wagner was very popular though not "at home" in Vienna. Those around Hanslick, who were setting the tone and opinion of Vienna, opposed Wagner and sided with musicians to whom Bruckner could not gain access. Thus the revolutionary, Bruckner, consistently sided with the equally revolutionary Wagner. We are fully justified in using the word "revolutionary," for the musical ideas of Bruckner's students rang in a new age in Vienna at the beginning of the 20th century. We should not view this as a threat but as a matter of course, for the musicians of whom we speak here were all, in their way, outsiders and stood as such outside the accepted norms. In their views, as well as their behavior, they did not fit into the accepted usual patterns or lifestyles of the good and respected citizen. But neither did the frivolous, fast-living, precocious Mozart, nor the quick-tempered, abrasive Beethoven. Nor could Schubert, who enjoyed a good time with his friends and drinking companions, be seen as a solid citizen but was, supposedly, given to "excesses."

Bruckner, after all, managed to join the faculty of Vienna University, became court organist and as such, a faithful servant of his emperor. He was granted an honorary degree by the University and, in his later years, lived in the Upper Belvedere Castle. He could therefore be regarded to be a tenant of His Majesty Francis Joseph I, and as such certainly a respected citizen. Yet at the same time he remained an outsider who often

Anton Bruckner's admiration for Richard Wagner had obvious reasons: Apart from similar musical ideas, the revolutionary role that Wagner played in conservative Vienna was a role also played by Bruckner. The silhouettes by Otto Böhler show Bruckner in a servile attitude taking snuff out of Wagner's snuff box. On the facing page, Bruckner is followed by the critics (headed by the all-powerful Eduard Hanslick and followed by Kalbeck and Heuberger), pictured as naughty little boys.

displayed the manners of a crude country cousin. He never gave up his demonstrative piety, was always glad to have a glass of wine with his students, among whom he preferred those who were willing to side with him and support him by promoting his works.

One could ignore all this, but it is best not to do so. After all, in every commentary on any of his symphonies it is made clear how much his students had participated in preparing the publication or had arranged the piano version of it, or made the composition more accessible and less "wild" by touching up the instrumentation or making cuts. If we say "less wild" we mean more acceptable to the public and, especially, shorter. The "monsters" that Bruckner presented to the public in his large symphonies, were, in later times, seen as having "sweep" and great breadth. When they were first performed they appeared to be oversized and beyond classical proportions. One technical issue must be mentioned. Like many other composers after him, Bruckner did not confine himself to the customary two themes or subjects to which composers of classic symphonies were expected to limit themselves. He set block of music upon block of music and, in doing so, overwhelmed his listeners with this abundance of themes. The public had been trained to follow a composer and think with him in the traditional manner. They did not recognize nor appreciate the fact that he pursued this way of composing as a worthy "successor" to Schubert.

Bruckner, the organist, was thoroughly acquainted with the rules of counterpoint, but in his improvisations on this king of instruments he also knew how to violate them with virtuosity. But it was difficult for him to develop his own concept of the symphony as is shown by the fact that he constantly revised, so that the various versions differed vastly one from another, not just in details. Even this fact can be interpreted in different ways. Some say it demonstrated his desire for perfection, others say it shows his basic and extreme uncertainty as a musician who never managed to master the forms.

A hundred years later a different opinion is held fairly unanimously. One views Bruckner as part of a great Austrian tradition and knows that he did not follow the line of Beethoven and Brahms, but that leading from Schubert to Gustav Mahler. And in doing so it is defensible to conclude that not all his work is masterful: Bruckner himself had reservations about many of his own works.

In his great Masses Bruckner also followed and perfected Schubert's work and certainly was inspired by the musical surroundings of his childhood. Not the narrow, strict confines of the Hofburgkapelle (The Court Chapel) where he officiated in Vienna, but the Monastery of St. Florian and its monumental monastery church—that is what one imagines before one's spiritual eye when one hears one of his Masses, though some musicians may frown on such visual images.

"Baroque" is the word often used when speaking of Bruckner's work. I prefer to call all his symphonies and Masses "Austrian," in the best sense of the word.

While most biographers contend that recognition came late and that appreciation of his works came slowly outside his homeland, this is only partly true. Bruckner not only had some students but also many enthusiastic followers, among whom we count Hugo Wolf and Gustav Mahler. Among his followers were such powerful writers as Max Graf, and many eminent conductors performed his works, including Franz Schalk.

That there were, on occasion, at the Vienna premiere of some of his works, brawls in the audience is, in our view, neither detrimental nor dishonorable. The history of modern music is full of such "scandals" when the conservative public, feeling insulted and provoked by the work performed, made its feelings known. Alban Berg and Igor Stravinsky, to mention but two very different composers, had their great moments of sensational scandals, about which those who were present talked for decades.

Another point deserving of consideration is that Brahms, purportedly Bruckner's outspoken critic, never uttered a derogatory comment about the "Master of St. Florian" during the latter's lifetime and was observed, as noted earlier, to be greatly moved during the elaborate funeral rites prepared for Bruckner.

Brahms was seriously ill himself at the time of Bruckner's death on October 11, 1896; he followed in April of the next year. With these two musicians gone the century came to an end musically in Vienna.

International recognition of Bruckner's symphonies was a slow process. A clear comprehension of his work only came through and after Gustav Mahler's symphonies. There were, of course, some performances of Bruckner's work outside Austria before that time, but aside from a small community of faithful in Holland, he was regarded for generations as a local hero and by no means as the universal master acknowledged today.

His great Masses, appropriate only on high holidays and requiring highly competent interpreters, remain to this day confined to Austria. The great changes in the liturgy of the Roman Catholic Church work against performances of Bruckner's Masses in church.

An annual festival, in existence for some years now in Linz, bears his name. A superb and notably successful concert hall was recently constructed to house these concerts. They are not confined to Bruckner's work but include works of other composers. An impressive number of world renowned orchestras bring their interpretations of Bruckner's work to Linz yearly. The recent edition of his complete works, carefully prepared over a period of decades, is a sure sign that he now is regarded as "established."

Gustav Mahler

Vienna may without compunction call itself the home of Gustav Mahler. Music historians referred to him for years as an Austrian conductor and composer, but recently the sequence of titles has been reversed—now designating him as an Austrian composer and conductor.

Mahler, born in Kalischt, Bohemia, on July 7, 1860, arrived in Vienna as a young student of music and soon came to regard the Imperial city as the only conceivable place to realize his ambitions. After finishing his studies at the Conservatory of Music "summa cum laude," he immediately turned to conducting "in the provinces" as was customary at that time to gain experience.

His career as a conductor was, above all else, purposeful: Via small Austrian theatres to Germany, via Prague and Budapest to Hamburg, and from Hamburg, at last, to Vienna and the Court Opera. Clearly this career was planned by a clever and alert, but, also an unusually gifted young musician. It almost goes without saying that Gustav Mahler, while "on his way" to Vienna, eagerly sought the backing of persons of wealth and rank, without whose support the highest musicial position in the old monarchy was beyond reach. He even embraced the Catholic faith, so that his Jewish origin would not prove a hindrance to his appointment to the service of His Apostolic Majesty.

Leonard Bernstein, widely regarded as one of the leading modern interpreters of Mahler's music, believes he has uncovered evidence which indicates that Mahler's conversion was virtually certain well before such a decision was necessary in the pursuit of his career. Even as a boy growing up in a Jewish family he appears to have demonstrated a great yearning for the glory of church music, associated as it was with a good deal of worldly appeal in the Roman Catholic monarchy.

There are indications that the musician Mahler hankered after things that were not in keeping with his position: For example as the Director of the Vienna Court Opera House, Mahler is reported to have had a great fondness for Franz Lehár's operettas, but because such stuff did not seem suitable for his professional library he secretly procured the scores for surreptitious study.

What is certain is that Mahler, after reaching his goal, was a powerful and extraordinary Director of the Court Opera. His correspondence, all of which is preserved in Vienna, documents not only his complete devotion to the Court Opera but also his skillful use of his position to help many composers.

It is said that Mahler ushered in a new era in the life of the Vienna Opera, and indeed brought about resplendent evenings of opera. Backed by heretofore unknown zeal and personal devotion, he raised the musical standards of this institution to quite astonishing heights. This excellence was in part due to the efforts of the architect Alfred Roller with whose cooperation Mahler introduced new scenic improvements. And in part it was due to his devotion to the encouragement of contemporary music—an undertaking more widely pursued then than today.

It was not in his nature to engage guest conductors of his own rank; and indeed as an interpreter he did not have the stature to invite competitors into his house. This is not an uncommon trait; we see it repeated in Vienna and elsewhere to this day. Unfortunately, such behavior sooner or later leads to tension and eventually to an explosion

GUSTAV MAHLER

DR O. BÖHLER'S SILHOUETTEN

While he was Director of the Court Opera in Vienna, Gustav Mahler reformed not only the style of performing in the House on the Ringstrasse. He also established a new style of conducting and astonished his orchestra and the public by his new language of gesture. Picture postcards, showing representative silhouettes, sold well at the time.

with the usual unhappy outcomes. Since Mahler's time Vienna's director/conductors, when they have completed their tour of duty, state that they were kicked out of the Vienna Opera, like their most famous predecessor. But they never make note of the fact that their most famous predecessor was much more than simply a fanatic Court Opera director.

Mahler, who had begun to compose long before his Vienna soujourn, was a musician whose work over the generations has been appraised quite variously. And indeed, in the second half of the 20th century he still was not regarded as fully "established." Only recently have several outstanding interpreters established his reputation as an accepted master.

His symphonies, all of which originally had some literary or poetic programs, overflowing into more and more exciting creations in which solo voices and massed choirs play a substantial part, are variously called symphonic cantatas or oratorios. Mahler scarcely had any time during the season to compose them; he used the summer months spent in the Austrian countryside to work on them. When composing them, he undoubtedly fell under the subconscious influence of those composers of whom he had been the enthusiastic interpreter. The contemptuous expression "Kapellmeistermusik" (music written by conductors, not composers) was ennobled by Mahler's symphonies once and for all. After him, composers like Anton von Webern openly admitted that they used effects they had discovered, in an operetta, for instance, at an opportune moment, but in such a way that no music lover could ever guess what the model was. These aspects of Mahler's works have hardly been investigated, and it is unlikely that anybody will do so in the near future. Yet, it is interesting to speculate on the idea that it is wrong to reproach a creative musician for having made use of one device or another, consciously or not, that elsewhere had a totally different meaning, but which served him well for his musical statement.

In Mahler's symphonies we easily recognize much of his background. We hear military band music, customarily played on official occasions. We hear Bohemian dance

GUSTAV MAHLER

DR. O. BÖHLER'S SILHOUETTEN

music and Viennese waltzes; we find literary references which were always important to him, and we discover his love for folk songs: he revives them, so to speak, and they turn up in his symphonies again and again.

To make things as simple as possible: Whatever Mahler composed was always "fractured," removed from the security of the established practice. It may end on a question mark, or is deliberately inconclusive like fragments or reminiscences of a once certain and secure world. We today can still identify and comprehend these reminiscences so clearly that wordy explanations are frequently by-passed by ordinary music-lovers who readily understand them without such learned exegeses.

At the turn of the century, however, Mahler was not so readily understood. He, too, had to depend upon his "apostles." On those occasions where he aroused real enthusiasm it was above all else due to the monumental aspect of his works. When his Symphony No. 8, called the "Symphony of the Thousand," at last had its famous first performance in Munich, both the public and the performers were overwhelmed by the shared monumental character of the experience.

After directing the Opera for 10 years composing all the while, the tension of two jobs became too much. He resigned his post in 1907 and went to New York to do some conducting there, promoting, among others, the symphonies of Anton Bruckner. He also wrote his last works. In 1911, after becoming well known and established in the U.S.A., he fell mortally ill and was forced to give up all engagements.

He returned to Vienna only in order to die in his city. Though he travelled relatively fast given the means available at the time, bulletins about his health were sent from every train stop. Thomas Mann, the writer, was particularly impressed by this triumphant return declaring that *Death in Venice* was inspired by Mahler's journey.

On May 18, 1911 Mahler died. He left a musical estate that was correctly assessed by the expert retained for probate. He wrote that at the moment no great monetary value could be assigned to his oeuvre, but that the next generation will most likely value it much more highly.

Alma Mahler, whom the composer had married in 1902, outlived her husband by several decades. She subsequently became the companion or wife of several important 20th-century figures, wrote a highly personal set of memoirs and edited, in a controversial selection, Gustav Mahler's letters. One is tempted to regard her as one of the founding members of that extraordinary club of widows of famous men that is still whispered and giggled about in musical circles.

The Viennese, blessed throughout the centuries with outstanding musicians, are all too familiar with such matters. The city's composers were always either unhappily married (and, with the exception of Haydn, were outlived by their resolute wives) or they remained, for a variety of reasons, unmarried, resulting in polite society gossip. Strangely enough no author has tried to ferret out the reason why many outstanding musicians remained unmarried—perhaps the examples of the marriages of their great predecessors instructed them.

But on to other matters more germane to this book. Above all else, one has to remember that Mahler's influence has lasted from 1911 to the present. The composers of the so-called Second Vienna School declared him, after some hesitation, to be their forerunner, but, by doing so, did in no way succeed in popularizing his symphonies with the broad public. Abroad, especially in Holland, Mahler was more often played than in Vienna, where people were inclined to speak of him as the former Director of the Court Opera. And further, Arnold Schönberg, Alban Berg and Anton von Webern were regarded as a "School" of their own.

The drastic upheavals following Hitler's rise to power greatly affected the musical world. Mahler's conversion to Catholicism meant nothing to the Nazis: he was branded as a Jewish "brain" musician and the performance of his works was "verboten." Elsewhere graver concerns than the promotion of Mahler's works preoccupied people. After World War II a Mahler "vogue" developed which continues to this writing. This interest was developed by conductors like Bruno Walter, who was a student and friend of Mahler's, and academics like Theodor W. Adorno, who made no secret of his reservations about Mahler, thereby arousing the sympathy and admiration of music lovers. Mahler's work was eventually introduced to a wider public which seems to admire him less as an innovator than as a spinner of fairy tales. The public appears to be less fascinated by the musical experiments to be discovered in his symphonies than by their beauty.

Arnold Schönberg and His School

The last world-wide revolution in music was derived entirely from Vienna as is shown by the labeling of composers who wrote this revolutionary music the "Second Viennese School."

Arnold Schönberg, generally regarded as the founder of this school, began as a composer of anything but revolutionary music. Born in 1874 in Vienna, he was first self-taught, then turned for lessons to Alexander von Zemlinsky, a respected, initially over-looked but recently rediscovered composer. Schönberg's early works are completely in the tradition of Brahms and Wagner. Schönberg always spoke and wrote of Brahms with the greatest respect and regarded himself as a composer within the great Western tradition, a posture little known nowadays.

In his youth, Schönberg was a bank clerk but occupied his spare time as a choral director. He augmented his income, as did many other important musicians after him, by writing the orchestration for operettas, as their composers at that time often had neither the time nor enough training to write out their full scores themselves. The division of labor in the U.S. manner, of handing what is called "sound" over to an expert, was not yet customary, but there were secret helpers.

At any rate, Schönberg was involved with every kind of music and practical music making, and was, when he moved to Berlin for the first time, in no way concerned with discovering new sounds. Instead he became the composer in residence of one of the well-known literary cabarets. On the side, he wrote his *Gurrelieder* (Songs of Gurre) which are oversized even by today's standards, but which attracted Richard Strauss' respect and landed him an appointment to teach composition at the Stern Conservatory in Berlin.

Schönberg belongs to that group of creative artists growing up at the beginning of the 20th century who, while making capital of their special ties to Vienna, tried to live and teach elsewhere, but always returned home—until the tragedy of our century made this impossible for them.

Not more than two years after his departure to Berlin, Schönberg was back in Vienna where he began teaching in a highly individual manner at a well-known "progressive" school and, more importantly, private students. Among these were Alban Berg, Anton von Webern, and Egon Wellesz, all of whom later became his most important supporters. The Chairman of the University's Department of Musicology, Guido Adler, took a quite unacademic and lively interest in the creative forces at work in Vienna. He supported Schönberg by sending to him his most gifted students. In doing so, he acted in a manner that seemed to him necessary and an action that in the Vienna of today must be viewed as a never repeated and quite remarkable event. More simply expressed: The gap between practice and research, between life at the university and live newly created music in today's Vienna is as wide and as deep as it is between a conservative public and the avant-garde musicians. One may reproach the public without fear of retribution, but not the academics who, in the last resort, are responsible for the teaching and training of the public: they are treated with reverence. In the Vienna of those last imperial years they thought more progressively than in our time.

While performances of Schönberg's works were not successful with the public before World War I, supporters believed that history would vindicate them. He and his

Arnold Schönberg (standing) and Alban Berg (center back, sitting) at a rehearsal of the Kolisch Quartet (1932). Drawing by Benedikt F. Dolbin.

students, Berg and Webern, caused "scandals," but their works were performed at the venerable hall of the Friends of Music by first-rank performers, led by the concertmaster of the Vienna Opera Orchestra and the Vienna Philharmonic Orchestra. Arnold Rosé, Gustav Mahler's brother-in-law and a figure whose name to this day is mentioned only with respect in the Vienna music world, participated in the first performances of Schönberg's works, save for *Pierrot lunaire.* The latter was written during the composer's second stay in Berlin and was first performed there.

Schönberg served in the Army during World War I. In 1918, after the downfall of the monarchy, and upon discharge, he founded a "Society for Private Musical Performances," run by him in an implacable, dictatorial manner. Schönberg and his students even forbade their audiences to applaud but did offer them a comprehensive cross-section of contemporary European music. In minutely and carefully prepared and rehearsed interpretations, often playing a work twice, they did not exclude any "school," not even opponents or competitors from their own city. They performed whatever had been recently composed. One of the consequences of these performances was that Schönberg was able to establish good contacts with numerous colleagues abroad. They in turn discharged their indebtedness to him by inviting him to give lectures and courses, thus making the world acquainted with his musical theories and his music.

Strictly speaking, Schönberg fared in much the same way as Haydn, but on a less conspicuous level. Haydn profited from performing the works of others not only as a Kapellmeister but also director of the Opera and concerts for Prince Esterházy. The difference, however, is easily described. The public of the early 20th century was not, as a matter of course, out to hear the latest music but rather had come to view these halls as musical museums. Those who attended Schönberg's concerts were chiefly colleagues, students and small groups of open-minded music lovers.

Only after 1921 did Schönberg develop what is known today as the "Twelve-Tone System" but which he called "Composition with Twelve-Tones that are related to one another." Should this system be seen as a democratization of musical material as was claimed? Schönberg's critics to this day point to the abolition of tonality that he brought about; yet his students reacted quite differently. Expressed in a simple way: while Alban Berg composed in accordance with Schönberg's methods he allowed himself whatever latitude seemed necessary to realize his artistic intentions. Anton von Webern, on the other hand, tried to extend this new democratization, and above all else, the strict rules that had been introduced by Schönberg, to *all* parameters of music. This departure led to "serial composition" to which, soon after World War II, a whole generation of composers declared themselves to be adherents, as Webern's followers.

Schönberg returned to Berlin in 1925 as the successor to Ferruccio Busoni, teaching the master class for composition of the Prussian Academy of Arts, and remained one of the leading international musical figures. What more can one say of a musician who held the most coveted of all teaching appointments?

That his compositions were not given a comparable status was, so to speak, a logical consequence of the conditions dominating European musical life touched upon earlier. That he continued to be identified as an Austrian musician is due to the fact that, on the one hand, he maintained close contacts with his Viennese master class students, and on the other, that the Viennese publisher Universal Edition continued to publish his music despite continuing financial losses. It must be noted with gratitude that Universal also published other ranking modern composers solely for reasons of prestige.

Schönberg's rôle as the father of a completely new school of music remains undisputed, although this music has not realized real public success. This failure reveals a deep misunderstanding of Schönberg's work. He began to compose in a late Romantic manner and for years only experimented with tonality of increasing complexity and tension. This exploration of tonality had preoccupied composers since Wagner and tonality finally fell apart in Schönberg's hands, so to speak. But his was not a destructive impulse for he sought and anticipated a new order and system in which no tone is subordinate to another. The system therefore contained at its core the potential for progress in a variety of directions.

He had hoped that the public would listen to and appreciate his music, in the same way they had come to the work of composers before him, and in this respect he was old-fashioned. But this reception was denied him, which led to great personal bitterness and intolerance. A public success like that of Berg's opera *Wozzeck* would have given him his greatest happiness. But he had to content himself with composing without compromise and with the knowledge that he had developed the rules that helped other musicians proceed.

Schönberg left Germany in 1933 for the United States where he taught and composed. His bitterness developed with his realization that his pivotal role as a composer did not result in popular acceptance. Again and again he vigorously rejected opinions, founded upon misunderstandings of what he was attempting, that viewed him as an ascetic theoretician. He ardently wished to reach the ordinary man and not to simply be remembered for his "method." In the end, though financially secure, he became a disgruntled, disappointed man, whose only remaining hope was to be appreciated and understood after his death.

After 1945 the Viennese failed, for many reasons, to recall the heroes who had been forced to emigrate. They found, in an embarrassed way, one excuse or another for paying homage only by offering decorations or other honors. But they took no positive steps to bring them back to the city—to become, as some feared, admonishing teachers or vengeful repatriates.

Schönberg died in 1951, the last of the Great Three of the Second Vienna School. Only then did a generation of young composers emerge who viewed this school differently and regretted that they had not been able to be in closer touch with the father of music of this century.

Schönberg had survived his two foremost students. The first, Alban Berg, was born in Vienna in 1885, a child of a wealthy family, a true Viennese, some would say, if only he had not been the composer of *Wozzeck*! Among his passions, aside from literature and music, were several pursuits that a true Viennese regards as worthwhile in life: Namely beautiful women, and soccer.

It may sound strange to raise such extra-musical interests in connection with the masters of this Second Viennese School. I do so because so little of them is known to the music lover, that these interests help flesh them out as human beings. Alban Berg was, then, not only a musician, but what they call in Vienna an eligible man about town and one of the loudest supporters at the soccer stadium, a man full of fiery passion. To turn to Schönberg for another: he was not only a composer, but also a passionate painter, inventor of exotic games and a good tennis player.

From 1904 on Berg was a student of Schönberg's. After a brief period in reduced circumstances he was able to study and compose without holding a job. Only after World War I did he have to earn some money as a teacher and coach in Schönberg's organization.

Berg had a kind of natural talent for composition, a fact that is rarely given any consideration. His first completed work, a piano sonata, shows great promise. His first work for the musical stage was *Wozzeck*, on which he worked for seven years from 1914 on. Three years were devoted to adapting the text and the composition of the music occupied him from 1917 to 1921. The opera was premiered by Erich Kleiber in Berlin in 1925. It is a master work of great coherence and integrity and was soon recognized as such.

Berg planned to base his second opera on Gerhard Hauptmann's *Und Pippa tanzt* (And Pippa dances) but was forced by the poet's demands for a very high royalty to look for another subject. He then developed the idea of compressing two of Frank Wedekind's dramas to form a single text for an opera to be called *Lulu*. After completing the first two acts and a "particell" (a short score in sketch form) for the third act he turned to the composition of his violin concerto. He had no idea what strange fate this opera would have half a century later.

The composer, who was seen by his contemporaries as the most sympathetic of the innovators, travelled much and liked to attend *Wozzeck* performances. He made in the course of those journeys friends and admirers throughout Europe and can be said to have remained more faithful to his teacher Schönberg than to his wife. She certainly knew of the passionate affair in which her husband had become involved, some of which was reflected in coded passages in his compositions.

When Berg died in 1935, Helene Berg took on, with an iron will and impressive consistency, the job of enhancing the reputation and advancing the work of her late husband. Not only her negotiations with her late husband's publisher, Universal Edition, but in dealings with his former friends she displayed a firmness of purpose that could not be ignored. She cut off in the bud any publication that might have been in any way detrimental to Berg. She forbade the completion of *Lulu* and in her will tried to prevent future efforts in that direction. She made scholarly attempts to write about Berg very difficult by denying access to his original letters and music manuscripts, allowing only the use of heavily censored editions which she made available. Berg's supporters respected her wishes,—thus Universal Edition delayed the publication of Friedrich Cerha's "integral" completion of *Lulu* until after her death in 1976.

It is clear that due to Helene Berg's determination posterity was forced to occupy itself with the existing and published works of Berg exclusively. As a result, his work came to be more highly esteemed than that of his teacher.

Anton von Webern, a lithograph by Hildegard Jone (1935). Conductor of the Workers' Symphony Orchestra, branded by the Nazis as "degenerate composer," Webern survived the Third Reich but was killed in a senseless accident in 1945.

Anton von Webern, the second great student of Schönberg, also died before the master. Webern was also born in Vienna (1883), but lived "in the provinces", before enrolling at the University in 1902, to study musicology. Guido Adler, the guiding light of the music department, encouraged him to study composition privately with Schönberg, whose student von Webern remained for the rest of his life.

After Webern had finished his studies in 1908 he was Kapellmeister in several small theaters, beginning a career as a conductor that did not get him as far as some of his admirers would later have liked to contend. After World War I he settled first in Vienna, then in Mödling near Vienna as a music teacher, composer and very busy conductor. From 1922 until 1934 he directed numerous performances of the Workers Symphony Concerts. This institution had been founded by the music critic and socialist, David Bach. Then as now, some possessed of high-minded but questionable views of workers education wished to give the working class access to what had been the artistic and aesthetic concerns of the bourgeoisie, without giving any thought to the appropriateness or relevance of the arts to their situation. Some of my readers may question introducing such a vexed political question into this book. I wish to point out that Webern did not offer the working class which had, until then, been excluded from most cultural life, simple or easily understood music, but rather "heavy fare." This is not to say that as a composer he considered presenting politically motivated music but rather that he presented music which even modern well-educated audiences find difficult to understand. The argument advanced by later composers like Hanns Eisler that the "proletarian" listener had to be educated step-by-step, was alien to the Vienna School.

Webern was most appreciated as a conductor for championing both contemporary music and politically for his efforts to promote the working class movement. He aimed only in part at a career as an internationally acclaimed symphony conductor in the traditional sense of the word. Such a role would not have fit with his stern nature and his unwillingness to compromise in matters of music.

Webern proved even more strict in musical matters than his revered master Schönberg. Even though he made no claim as a musical revolutionary, he was, nevertheless, the most consistent composer of this "School": indescribably lucid and strict in his manner of working, aiming for such concentration and conciseness that many of his "pieces" consist of only a few bars. His posthumous scores contain fragments which are meant to be played in sequence and convey to the listener the same impression conveyed by the completed pieces,—a highly concentrated form of musical thought.

Yet Webern was, like his master, completely convinced that he was only fostering strict technique in order to restore purity to music. Serial technique appeared to him as full of color, poetry and atmosphere. We might compare Webern's music to a highly polished gem which by being flawless and untouchable attracts ever greater admiration.

That Webern lived, not in Vienna, but in nearby Mödling, need not lead to the conclusion that he was anything other than a Viennese musician. He simply enjoyed more peace and quiet there, with his modest means managed a little better, and when as a former Socialist he was no longer encouraged or supported by the pre-Hitlerite fascist regime, he was somewhat "out of range." He remained there throughout World War II, supported by Universal Edition, respected by musicians as an authority, and left in peace by the powers that were.

He died in 1945, after the end of the war, in a frighteningly senseless way. While taking refuge with his brother-in-law and his family in Mittersill (Salzburg province), he was shot by an American soldier due to a misunderstanding during a military police action against black marketeers.

And again we come back to the amazing story of the three composers and their "effect upon music." Though Schönberg developed his new method of composition years ago, the world of music has not uniformly accepted it. Musicians worked and experimented with this entirely novel means of dealing with tonal material, and a kind of international alliance of composers seemed to evolve. But music lovers in general did not join them. If the latter sided with anybody they did so with Alban Berg, a composer with a human side. They remained completely puzzled by Webern's work, though he managed to inspire a whole generation of significant composers around the world. Men like Pierre Boulez, Karlheinz Stockhausen, Bruno Maderna, Luigi Nono and many others have called themselves sons and grandsons of Webern, yet Webern's music and that of his successors has not found its way to public acceptance. The time when music of a given period was readily accepted by audiences of the time has long passed.

After musicians the world over have identified the works of Schönberg, Berg and Webern as important, Vienna has begun to acquaint itself with them, even though with an air of puzzled pride. Appropriate anniversaries are being celebrated and the great concert establishments are making distinct efforts to keep their music before the public. There is as yet, in all honesty, no genuine affection among the general public for these masters, but the blind and prideful affection showered on many masters of the past by the Viennese would make little sense for the masters of the Second Vienna School.

The Brothers Schrammel

In any good and proper music city the link between what is today called "serious" music and what, for a very long time, has been called folk or popular music, is intact. That is to say: The composers and performers of both kinds know each other and ideally esteem each other as experts in their respective endeavors.

Vienna has always excelled in this collaboration. From time immemorial those who came to town to sing or play for gentlemen of the court have also sought and often received approval by the broad public. Indeed in the last two centuries emperors, sometimes themselves composers, presented their glittering spectacles not only for themselves and their illustrious guests, but also and almost as a matter of course for the Viennese public. No stigma was attached to the Viennese composer who made his way from the Court Theater at the Kärntnertor to the stages of the suburbs. The public, even high society, attended the suburban performances, not considering it below their dignity to see with great pleasure and understanding a new farce or a successful magic play.

After the Biedermeier or Pre-March days (the terms vary according to one's political point of view), that is to say around the middle of the 19th century, it was clear that the nobility and the church were no longer the only protectors and patrons of the arts. The rich and rising bourgeoisie of the *Gründerzeit* (age of industrial development), ambitious entrepreneurs, wished to present themselves as equally important in their support of the arts. The age of the city's spectacular growth, the period of the great entrepeneurs, the time of The World Exhibition, was that splendid interval when music was a matter that brought all of Vienna together, because it was equally important to every class of citizen.

The waltz that, two generations earlier, had been regarded as a dance of the lower classes and frowned upon because it was vulgar and erotic was no longer called folk music. Now, the expression "folk music" was the equivalent of what is still today called by the strange term "Schrammel" music.

This term is strange, because on the one hand it is an all-embracing term for entertainment music for singers and small instrumental ensembles, and on the other, because it is the only correct term for a quite different and unique kind of music, namely the music the two brothers Josef and Johann Schrammel composed and played with their partners from 1877 on.

Whether one should present the life of the Schrammel Brothers in a book such as this is problematic. They were children of humble folk, they both learned to play the violin and might have become respected members of the Vienna Philharmonic Orchestra. But they both decided, after having finished their studies at the Conservatory, to become entertainment musicians. They played in tavern gardens, first in a trio, then a quartet. In this they were the legitimate heirs of the small ensembles at the time of Johann Strauss the Elder and Joseph Lanner. And also like Strauss and Lanner they were, of course, prepared to compose much of their own music.

They were never unique in the strictest sense of that word, for similar groups could be found in virtually every Viennese tavern. Vienna and its suburbs contained many a tavern garden and open-air drinking establishment, all marked by a bunch of greenery on a pole outside the front door. There vintners were allowed to sell their own wine at cer-

This copper engraving from the magazine Der Eipeldauer *(the name suggests a country yokel atmosphere) that was widely read at the time, shows a scene from the social life of Vienna in 1817. A Biedermeier party wines and dines and dances waltzes with only one harp player and one fiddler as a band.*

tain times of the year, a privilege granted to them by imperial patent. Almost all of these establishments, and particularly those located in the traditional vineyard areas, and in the Prater, the famous woods next to the World Exhibition grounds, provided musical entertainment, in order to compete with their neighbors. So there were a great number of such little ensembles, many duos and sometimes what was called, at that time, folk song societies: ensembles of a few popular singers and entertainment musicians providing either a whole evening's entertainment or sometimes circulating from one place to another presenting short guest performances.

Such groups always featured a male or female singer, the songs of the lady, strangely enough, being slightly wilder and cruder in both subject and song texts than those of their male colleagues. Reading the several histories of these Viennese folk singers which contain the lyrics of the risqué songs awash with double-entendre and presented by the most popular of these female interpreters, even today's reader will be astonished, for there is rarely anything like them in our liberated and immoral present. The singers, in accordance with their taste or importance, were accompanied either by a single instrumentalist or by an ensemble.

Their lives seem to have followed a standard pattern. They were fêted as folk heroes, became very rich, had admirers in all circles of society and to a person squandered their riches. None of them were prepared to cope with their newly found wealth, nor with the demands of their jobs, so they died in poverty, their former admirers unwilling to come to their aid. But after their death their names reappeared to be included in the ample store of Viennese legends.

The brothers Schrammel, however, were not to function as accompanists but to specialize in making their own form of Viennese music with their special brand of instrumentation. The typical "Schrammel Quartet" consisted of: two violins (required for all forms of Viennese music, to play in "blissful thirds"); accompanied by a contra guitar, or later an accordion, one of those sometimes called "button concertina," more complicated to play than today's accordion, which offers a piano keyboard to the right hand; and as the fourth instrument and used exclusively in the Schrammel Quartet, the so-called "picksüsse Hölzl", ("gooey little woodwind") a very small clarinet which produces a very piercing, loud, but also jolly sound.

This little clarinet is the most important instrument in the "classic" Schrammel Quartet, and anyone telling a visitor that it can be done without, is wrong. Indeed genuine "Schrammelmusik" can only be made by a group which includes a competent player of this difficult instrument who knows the old music.

The success of the brothers Schrammel was instantaneous and overwhelming. Soon after their first appearance their reputation spread throughout the city drawing the public to the taverns in which they played. They played faster than other groups, even in the most elegant circles into which they were increasingly invited, not just by the nobility but by members of the imperial family as well, to provide the musical entertainment for their soirées. Soon thereafter they were invited to tour, by crowned heads who had heard them in Vienna and wanted to receive them back at home. Such was the enthusiasm that surrounded their music.

Serious musicians also admired the music of the brothers Schrammel. Hans Richter, the prominent conductor of Wagner's music dramas, invited the Vienna Philharmonic Orchestra at the close of a season to join him at a "Heurigen" where the Schrammel Band was playing, saying that he could offer nothing better to his admired orchestra. The leading Viennese violinists listened to and played with their colleagues in the entertainment world, a practice which continues to this day. Indeed one of the present-day Schrammel Quartets includes the first violinist and clarinetist of the Philharmonic Orchestra—perhaps the most sophisticated ensemble in all of Vienna.

At some time before the obligatory tragic end of the brothers Schrammel, who died early and poor, the family name had become a kind of brand name for a type of music. When the Viennese speak of *Schrammelmusik* they mean the Viennese folk music that is still played in restaurants and "Heurigen." One adds luster to the reputation of a good interpreter of this folk music by styling his ensemble with his own name, to which the word "Schrammel" is added, as if the Schrammels had never existed as human beings, but were only two fiddles, a clarinet and a bass instrument. And even the Schrammel repertoire, their music itself, has endured the same fate. Many dances, songs and marches were originally composed by Johann or Josef Schrammel, which a real Viennese still knows, but only the expert will know the actual composers. As time went on, almost all Viennese light music for small ensembles, from duos to quartets, was simply called "Schrammelmusik."

It is as rewarding to the friend of genuine and therefore long-lived folk music to search for the compositions of the brothers Schrammel and their many arrangements of other composers' music, as it is to seek out opportunities to hear original Schrammel music today.

If and when we hear it, we will understand, on the one hand, the enthusiasm of yesteryear, for it is very ingenious and everything but simple music. Yet on the other hand, we will begin to appreciate at what a high level that which is called musical instinct operated in those days in Vienna. The connoisseurs who met at the Schrammel taverns were largely simple folk and included horse cab drivers who were reputed to be particularly musical. But equally welcome as casual guests were the aristocrary. They were not looking for vulgar entertainment, but supported and promoted "Schrammelmusik" with their money and prestige.

When trying to create an impression of the "good old times", an author must remain silent about mismanagement, poverty and misery in order to deliver the desired picturesque result. However when writing on music in Vienna this author can honestly report that only quality was regarded highly, and that it was appreciated by rich and poor alike.

Two minor Viennese musical subjects can rightfully be included in this essay on Schrammel music, although they could as easily be dealt with in separate chapters.

There is, first of all, Viennese theater music, which has a lot to do with popular folk music and which is recognized wherever plays by Raimund and Nestroy are given with the original music. An easily proved connection obtains between comedy songs with roots in Baroque Jesuit Theatre, and true, popular Viennese street songs. It was from this treasure chest of tunes that much theater music came.

Secondly, we must note the unique Austrian military music which as in other parts of the world serves for marching as well as for the display of worldly power. But, in the City of Music, it had to have special qualities. The conductors of the more famous military bands of the Austro-Hungarian Monarchy always became Kings of the Waltz or composers of operettas. They were certainly not soldiers, though they all had a strict, thorough, traditional musical training. Many of them became quite famous—Carl Michael Ziehrer or Franz Lehár, and some, though their names are forgotten, live on through their waltzes which remain in the musical memory of every Viennese, just as surely as do those of their immortal competitors.

Again the close ties between the music of soldiers and ordinary people and the highest forms of serious music are easily traced. In Gustav Mahler's symphonies, for instance, military music often appears in the background. Sometimes he even writes into his scores "like a military funeral procession," which reaffirms that some of Mahler's inspiration reaches back to his youth when he ran behind a marching military band playing fiery martial music or a slow funeral dirge.

All this is quite simply related to our subject. In Vienna music of all kinds always had to maintain a certain standard and was an art respected and loved by all. Even today we Viennese live by those standards.

The Viennese Popular Song

One can trace the history of Viennese folk music by relating it to the brothers Schrammel or to Viennese popular song and its interpreters. But in so doing we shall have occasion to mention others who are no longer familiar, even to the Viennese. Familiar or unfamiliar, both song composers and their interpreters are in a real sense anonymous heroes who have to resign themselves to anonymity while their creations live on as folk songs.

Several devoted Viennese have carefully collected and published editions of these folk songs and assiduously ferreted out the names of many of their composers. So, the anonymity suggested above is not absolute. Thus one can readily ascertain the author of the text and music of the "Fiakerlied", the Hungarian Alfred Pick, who migrated to Vienna but lacked the training to write down the music for his own song. He whistled the tune for a friend who wrote down the music, and the Viennese now regard it as immortal. We also have the special case of the "whistling composer" who was blessed with brilliant song ideas but refused to learn his trade as a composer, yet has been more successful than many a "learned" composer.

And yet: Such examples are the exception which proves the rule that the most popular Viennese songs were created by serious musicians.

Max Graf, the critic who was mentioned earlier and who knew Bruckner and Brahms and all the musicians following them, was my teacher. May he forgive me if I turn to him again to provide my readers with a few composers and song titles from his book. His criterion for selecting these songs and composers was to choose those that had survived and which he thought would survive for decades.* Johann Schrammel ("The Heart of a Real Viennese"); Karl Lorens ("Well, Let's Go Out to Nussdorf", "Let's Drink Another Little Bottle", "Humans, Humans We All Are", "Farewell, Old Times"); Alexander Krakauer ("You Kind-Hearted Father in Heaven", "My Love Lives on the Banks of the Danube"); Johann Sioly ("The Deutschmeister Military Band is Here", "Today I am Already Tipsy", "Because I'm an Old Imbiber", "No Goethe Wrote This"); Rudolf Sieczynski, ("Vienna, Vienna Only You Alone", "In Grinzing at the Heurigen"); Ludwig Gruber ("My Mom was Viennese", "There Still Will be Wine to Drink"); Franz Böhm ("In the Leimgrube and in Wieden"); Alfred Kmoch ("Nightly Drinking Parties, That's My Life"); Alexander Hornig ("Little Bird, You Fly Out into the World"); Viktor Korzhe ("Come, Come, Little Joe, Don't Talk"); Hans Kutschera ("Do You Know Mom What I Dreamt?"); Wilhelm Wiesberg ("They Kept Us in the Army"); Carl Michael Ziehrer ("Oh Vienna, My Dear Vienna"); Gustav Wanthaler ("Look! He Rides a Bike"); Theodor Woltitz ("Roan, Roan Don't You Dare!"); Johann F. Schild ("That's the Way of a Viennese"); Julius Stern ("This is True Viennese", "When the Swallows Come Back Again They'll Be Surprised"); Georg Schiemer ("On the Water, On the Water, That's Where I am at Home"); Edmund Eysler ("Only a Viennese Girl Can Kiss Like That").

This list, appearing in Graf's book, now out of print, is dear to me, because it is an endless source of information for anyone interested in the subject of Vienna, City of

---

*Most of the song titles or first lines are, in the original, in broad Viennese dialect and translated here into English as literally as is possible.

Music. It is quite incomplete. Particularly it does not take account of those still living composers whose contributions to Viennese popular music can only be assessed when one must write their obituaries and so must laboriously seek out the songs they wrote.

Much might be recounted about many of these composers, and some of the song texts must be explicated so that not only the foreigner but also the Viennese can understand where their particular charms lie. Other songs not mentioned might also be singled out for special recognition, in order to make it clear how musicians of uncomplicated minds and frequently little theoretical training managed to reach deeply into the mysterious realm of melody and song that has its center somewhere in the heart of Vienna.

All these songs were created quickly and became popular overnight, and that without the technology of mass media publicity we know today. As soon as they were recognized as "special" their fame spread throughout the city. Such rapid dissemination was in part due to a group of very popular restaurant and tavern players and singers who were professionally involved in learning and performing the latest hits. But also it was due to the many "natural" singers and "whistlers," amateurs who performed at night while holding very pedestrian daytime jobs, yet were able to entertain the public as well as their professional colleagues.

A "natural singer" needs no lengthy explanation: a good singer without proper training. But what about a "whistler"? Well, at the turn of the century there were music makers who whistled so charmingly that they were accompanied by the proverbially sweet sound of the violin. This form of artistry is almost forgotten today. However, one old man can still be seen roaming the streets accompanying himself on a "button accordion" and whistling the old melodies. The young people who today play as street musicians in "Pedestrians Only" zones, so as not to be deprived of their rights for street music making, call him respectfully by his professional name "The Little Lark from Hernals." Of course, he is not the first Viennese whistler artist of that name, but he may be the last, for while some very young Schrammel music groups exist, there do not seem to be any young whistling artists around any longer.

A marginal note: Singers of Viennese songs still perform today. They have their public and their own hang-outs. With any luck one can discover them for oneself in some eating establishments on certain days, but better ask some connoisseurs when and where these "natural" singers perform. They have nothing in common with the professionals who perform every night in the taverns around Vienna and in the city itself. The former know songs and texts that are hardly noted down anywhere, and above all, they are unwilling to become a marketable commodity. They proudly carry on an old folk tradition and have no interest in becoming well-known. They confine themselves to a small circle of friends and an atmosphere of quiet intimacy that should not be invaded by the record industry or any other form of mass media.

One can learn from them how the Viennese sang once upon a time: With considerable soulfulness and great *sentiment*. The word "sentimentality" does not adequately describe it; it is mellower still, even more tearful, close to a mood that modern man finds hard to tolerate. Alternatively it has a lot of verve, one might say, aggressiveness that occasionally borders on vulgarity or cruelty, extensive and frightening, and yet part of an important tradition. Some Viennese female folk singers—including some of the most popular—were noted not only for appearing in men's clothes, but also for the forthright vulgarity of their songs.

And misinterpretations have crept into our understanding of these songs, not just at the hands of foreign guests. There is for example, the *alte Drahrer*—the "old imbiber" whom every Viennese would instantly define as a man who drinks as often as he can, i.e., a man who is at least out for a good time if not an alcoholic. This "old imbiber" was, when

Entertainment in Vienna before the March revolution. A male singer is accompanied by a female harp player as he sings "couplets." Some were so provocative that the Metternich censorship forbade their performance, yet there always were singers and instrumentalists ready to do so. No restaurant owner could afford to do without this form of entertainment or music.

the song named after him was composed, nothing more than an organ grinder ("drahn"—Viennese dialect verb for "to turn a handle"), as is clear from performances by early interpreters. Only later was the original meaning of that word forgotten, and today "the old imbiber" is still an old crony even though there are again a lot of organ grinders about.

Or the reader may wish to turn to a long passage from a novel by Hans Weigel, in order to comprehend how much of Viennese worldly wisdom and philosophy is incorporated in the text of a little song: "Only when everything will be over, when there will be no music and no wine, then I'll pack up everything, no sooner. Only when the music stops that we Viennese love so much . . ." Weigel drew our attention to the relative importance of things for the typical Viennese: First there has to be music, and that in the form of Viennese violin music, and then wine is mentioned, but not much wine, or drinking a great deal of it, only the idea of a "good drop", of good quality. Only then does the song mention the Viennese girls who always go with having a "good time."

All the songs enumerated here contain a good deal more patriotism than the "homeland songs" of other places. They are proof of the fact that the poet and/or composer of a Viennese song is "at home" in the city, often localizing his patriotic sentiments in a particular neighborhood of the city, and by implication that modern idea of a mobile society, of frequently pulling up roots, is alien to the "Weltanschauung" of the Viennese. Furthermore, all these songs also have a preoccupation with death which is as true of the oldest examples as those of our day. They reveal that the true Viennese has always thought of his mortality, his death, and wishes to face this event with dignity and composure, even to having some control in the matter. It should be noted that this concern for death is more evident in Viennese songs than those of other areas or nations.

But to get back to the popularity of these songs: They were either composed for folk song groups who made them known as they toured the city, or they were sung by individual well-known interpreters and immediately taken up by the public and carried from one tavern and from one part of the city to another. In a musical city like Vienna, this simplest of all distribution methods was amazingly effective at a time when copyright was hardly thought of.

Admittedly the city was more actively concerned with music then than it is today; there were more people making music than we can imagine. At the time of Schubert, it was a matter of course that every teacher had to train his little flock of students in music just as thoroughly as in other subjects, for the educated person was expected to possess a reasonable music training.

One additional observation: The folk singers, who are lumped here in a quite anonymous way, because their names would, after all, only mean something to experts, were the heroes of all classes of Viennese society including the ranks of the nobility. They were regularly invited into the homes of the nobility where they were treated as highly esteemed artists, not exotic animals. Antonia Mansfeld, for example, notorious for appearing in men's clothes with a repertoire that could only be called rather risqué, was asked, during the World Exhibition in 1873, to sing for prominent guests of the city. The brothers Schrammel frequently performed for the highest society circles and received numerous gifts from foreign monarchs for performances initiated by Austria's archdukes to demonstrate for their dignitaries what was meant by the Viennese love of music. The troupe of folk singers around Johann Fürst was especially patronized by Princess Pauline Metternich who recommended many artists to patrons abroad and saw to it that they were invited to many of the grand festivities in Vienna. And (I realize that I am giving more than one example) the Vienna folk singer Mitzi Turecek entered the annals of music history as "Fiakermilli" (The Cab Driver's Girl) for she was the center of attraction at cab driver's dances. She later appeared as one of the main characters in the second act of *Arabella*, the opera for which Hugo von Hofmannsthal wrote the text and Richard Strauss the music.

If we endeavor to view the present from a certain perspective, very little has changed since then. To this day a few of the old bards of Viennese song enjoy the respect of all. They know how to compose a good Viennese song, and thanks to today's copyright laws some quickly do well, as a good new song becomes popular throughout the town.

And yet, the composers, unless they are their own interpreters as well, often remain almost unknown. We hardly know their names, their songs are quickly accepted as "traditional", and virtually no one is abashed by such a course of events. A good song is the property of all, the property of the City of Music. The only condition is payment of royalties, for no music can be performed without giving the composer his due, which was not the case in bygone days.

Highly localized censorship applicable in one or the other specific Viennese districts (which was still the case at the end of the 19th century) has disappeared. In the times of the folk song troupe of Fürst, of the well-known Edmund Guschelbauer, of the famous Mansfeld, we know that some songs of a critical or vulgar approach were not allowed to be sung in all of Vienna. As at the time of Prince Metternich of Vienna Congress days, they had to pass some minor official of the censorship department, and if he happened to be in a bad mood one tried to get it passed in another district.

The present popularity of the old Viennese song can best be judged by the fact that the lords of the Viennese musical world, that is, members of the Vienna Philharmonic and the leading members of the Vienna State Opera, do not think it below their dignity to perform these songs publicly and usually to great success. Some members of the Vienna *Burgtheater*, bent on penetrating the realm of their musical colleagues, also have become interpreters of Viennese songs.

Perhaps I should mention some modern Viennese singers, without, I hope, causing anger or jealousy among their competitors: The unforgettable Hans Moser, whom no one has yet succeeded in out-shining, sang both old and new Viennese songs. Another who has as yet found no successor is Nagl Maly, the resolute Viennese songstress, with a voice that reminded one of a raucous cello. But we can be certain these two together with many others who have not been mentioned here, will one day have their successors. For this kind of music is still alive and flourishing in the city.

Franz Lehár and the Silver Age of Operetta

Exactly at the turn of the century the brief, but great era of classical operetta came to an end. Johann Strauss, Junior was dead, and in 1899 Karl Millöcker, who was recognized as the second greatest operetta composer, also died. Connoisseurs in Vienna were united in their opinion of the meaning of Millöcker's death in their obituaries: The great times were past and anything composed and performed thereafter would be second-rate and above all, less elegant.

Friends of operetta never shared this opinion, yet a majority of critics, including the most powerful, have to this day continued in this verdict which the evidence supports. The world-wide successes of subsequent Viennese operettas have not tarnished the luster of *Fledermaus, Gasparone, The Gypsy Baron* and *The Beggar Student.* Rather these operettas have always been regarded as belonging to the "Silver Age of Operetta." It makes no sense to try to revise this long established assessment. Moreover, the most important light opera masters of that time saw no reason to object to being grouped together as Masters of the Silver Age of Operetta. If some—like Franz Lehár—were, in their hearts, unhappy about such a verdict and truly intended to do something more than simply turn out popular operettas, we need note this only in passing, for history has closed the case and the assessment stands.

The most important name, Franz Lehár, has already been mentioned. He was born in Komorn in Hungary in 1870, studied at the Prague Conservatory, became a fully trained violinist and composer and began his career as a military band master in Pola, Trieste, Budapest, and Vienna. These were the same type of stations that a "serious" composer would have gone through. As a military band master, of course, Lehár was anything but a soldier. He was in the happy situation of always having bands at his disposal for which he could compose, and not only military marches. For the monarchy military bands were constantly used as great entertainment orchestras and had to supply not simply band music, but quite ambitious programs for a sophisticated public.

One must not forget that in the last decade of the 19th century there were no clear indications of the possibility of a major war. The military were therefore regarded as a kind of wonderful toy of the Emperor, one that served as a unifying instrument of the monarchy, and was representative of the greatness and glory of the empire. Military band leaders were under just as close scrutiny by the musical world as were entertainment musicians of the caliber of the Strauss family. Their marches as well as their waltzes could just as easily become the hits of the season, so it was the ambition of every composing band master, first to get a job in Vienna and then to become famous in a musical world that was anything but military.

Franz Lehár managed to obtain that favored spot. Beginning in 1902 he had composed in only three years six operettas that were performed in Vienna. He was a known, though not yet famous musician. Then, in 1905, his *Merry Widow* became a triumph and brought him into the limelight. The story of the first performance and the growing success of this operetta has always remained the talk of the town in Vienna, and has the characteristics of a fairy tale. The libretto of the *Merry Widow* had been handed over to the critic and composer Richard Heuberger (of *Der Opernball* fame) who had started to write some music for it. Then Lehár became interested in the subject and urgently requested to be

A caricature of Franz Lehár from 1933. He was at that time not only world-famous, but bulging with royalties. The loyal chroniclers of Viennese operetta confirm that Lehár enjoyed an extraordinary position among entertainment musicians. Indeed: Once when the Vienna State Opera was in financial difficulties they even decided to put his Giuditta *in their repertoire.*

allowed to have a go at it. Upon its completion a large group of libretto writers and publishers were only mildly impressed by Lehár's music for the *Merry Widow* when they heard it.

For Christmas, 1905 the management of the Theater an der Wien put the operetta on after only a brief rehearsal period and on a shoestring. They were of the opinion that it would be only a short-lived success, lasting a few weeks. They remained of this opinion after the first performance. A few weeks and a shower of free tickets later the great turn-around suddenly came for reasons that are not quite clear even today. Suddenly everybody was of the opinion that the *Merry Widow* was the best operetta of the budding century.

Lehár had won the game and remained, for the rest of his life, the unrivaled king of the operetta stage. Not only in Vienna, where the *Merry Widow* ran for years, but also abroad where it gained great audiences, it enjoyed a popularity that was not diminished but rather seemingly increased by the arrival of silent and sound film.

Lehár, of whose works we mention only two, no longer composed in a typical Viennese style; but—as it was soon called—in a Hungarian manner. The waltz, no longer the essential ingredient of his operettas, was replaced by other folkloristic flavors. More importantly, he used a more mundane musical language, international rather than national in style.

The second Lehár world-wide success was *The Land of Smiles* or, as it was first called, *The Yellow Jacket*. Again it was not an immediate success but after revision joined the ranks of the *Merry Widow*. The other, *Giuditta*, was at first intended to be an opera, not an operetta, and so gives us some insight into the limitations which Lehár was unable to overcome. He had intended to write a colorful opera, but in 1934, when the work was ready to be premiered, the finances of the Vienna State Opera were so bad that the management was actually ready to accept it in this holiest of holies. But the musical world recognized it as an unsuccessful hybrid of opera and operetta despite the fact that it was from the hands of a world-famous composer who counted among his personal friends Giacomo Puccini, and among his enemies Richard Strauss. Lehár in time reluctantly had to admit that he had perhaps bitten off more than he could chew.

From the turn of the century on Lehár and his colleagues—who will have to be briefly mentioned here—enjoyed a kind of lifestyle that today goes by the name of "old Austrian." They lived in big houses in Vienna; composed and discussed affairs in the coffee house; had villas for the summer months in Ischl, where the Emperor resided during the season; their lavish entertaining was carefully followed by the public. They attributed much importance to titles, honors, and decorations and paid great attention to the business side of their writing. On the side they composed, secretly or openly, music which brought in no money. They adjusted to the political situation: During World War I they wrote many patriotic operettas that were immediately forgotten. In short they clung to their lifestyle by any means available for as long as they could.

Franz Lehár remained a greatly revered and much played composer, even during the time of the Nazi regime in Austria, and thought nothing of making arrangements with those in power. Many of his colleagues had to emigrate and died either abroad or, forgotten and disappointed, upon their return home after 1945. It must be assumed that at least some of them might have preferred to stay with Lehár in Ischl, rather than emigrate, if this had not been made impossible by the racial teachings of the National Socialists. The progeny of these composers may not wish to admit it, but there is no proof that, apart from Robert Stolz, a single leading entertainment musician emigrated from Austria a day earlier than was absolutely necessary. They all lived as long as it was possible in their world of operetta.

The mention of names may seem like a very personal choice, but that is a risk one must take. Oscar Straus succeeded in creating a masterpiece without parallel. Following the success of the *Merry Widow* Straus, in Berlin at the time, announced that he was going to write a similarly successful operetta. He composed *Walzertraum* (Dream of Waltzes) which was indeed successful on first staging. From 1907 on this work was a serious competitor for the *Merry Widow* and has been ever since, at least in Vienna.

Oscar Straus is a good example of those composers who lived exclusively in the world of operetta. He made music in Berlin until the rise of National Socialism made it clear that there was no place for him there. He returned to Vienna where he stayed until 1938 when he was forced to emigrate, first to Paris, then New York and finally Hollywood—the classical route of refugees. He mostly composed discreet waltzes and little operettas in which, in contrast to Lehár, the Viennese waltz was the central element. Among his other works the public at large still knows is his music for Max Ophüls' film version of Arthur Schnitzler's *Merry-go-round* (La Ronde). After World War II he returned to Europe and died in Bad Ischl, the summer resort of the masters of the Silver Age of Operetta. He had lived six years longer than Franz Lehár.

The next really popular composer who must be mentioned is, without any doubt, Emmerich Kalman, though for musical reasons, I think a composer like Leo Fall more important. Born at Olmütz in 1873, student of respected teachers who, by chance, were both named Fuchs, and who were teaching theory and composition at the Vienna Conservatory, Leo Fall became, first of all, Kapellmeister in Germany, moved to Vienna in 1906 and decided to devote himself exclusively to composition. In 1907 he wrote an operetta *The Merry Farmer* which was not premiered in Vienna and, moreover, did not have Vienna or Budapest or any other city as the place of action, but rather a village. He became a highly successful composer with this, the first "farmyard" operetta. Yet he was always in financial troubles so was compelled to write operetta after operetta in order to maintain his lifestyle. He died in 1925 and so was spared the miseries of his colleagues.

The "Masters of the Silver Operetta" were the subject of countless caricatures. When portrayed as a "Salon Concert Band", it certainly made sense, for, in the end, they all made music together. This sketch from 1912 shows from left to right: Edmund Eysler, Oscar Straus, Oscar Nedbal, Franz Lehár, Carl Michael Ziehrer, and Leo Fall.

His brother Richard, who also was a composer and already working in Hollywood before the Nazis, happened to be in Europe during the bad times. As far as is known, he was put to death in Auschwvitz in 1943.

In addition to Emmerich Kalman and Edmund Eysler, Robert Stoltz was also one of this group of composers, but he became well-known only after the sound film became popular. Later he achieved some recognition by virtue of his extreme old age and by the fact that as a composer and conductor he was a kind of relic of those glorious times. They all are, by their names and their fates, the last representatives of that short-lived glory of Viennese operetta, the last musical link between Johann Strauss and the musical.

There are easily reconstructed links, hardly known to the public: Example: The father of the composer of *My Fair Lady* Frederic Loewe, was a tenor at the Theater an der Wien who was present at the premiere of the *Merry Widow*, the only work the world-wide success of which can be compared to that musical. The son of this man, who had been trained during the Silver Age of Viennese operetta, thus wrote what was more or less the last "American" operetta which in Europe was already considered a "Musical."

One can easily understand that the fate of these composers not only depended on their success with their operettas but also on everything connected with it. There were, during the first third of the 20th century, those legendary theater directors who made a fortune, if they found the "right man" but occasionally also went bankrupt after a flop. There were amazing connections between agents, literary people and libretto writers, who were not really writers but hacks. The success of a new operetta often depended upon a few famous, sometimes world-famous interpreters who therefore insisted upon being taken seriously. There was luxury and bankruptcy. Some clever musicians self published their wares to produce additional income.

Moreover, there were proven and unproven collaborations about which rumors float around Vienna to this very day. Again, just two examples. There is the wonderful story about the great violinist Fritz Kreisler to whom, over a cup of coffee, Hugo von Hofmannsthal made a gift of the text for his musical *Sissy*. According to another version Hofmannsthal suggested to Richard Heuberger much earlier the line "Come with me to the *chambre séparée* [private room in a café or inn]. The fact remains that these people knew and esteemed each other, met regularly in their favorite cafés and talked to each other. They knew that something like a copyright existed, but helped each other occasionally with a line or an idea.

The second example is known to everybody: It concerns that widely successful operetta: *The White Horse Inn* (Im Weissen Rössl), a musical comedy by the composer Ralph Benatzky who was born in Mährisch-Budwitz in 1884, and was a student of the famous conductor Felix Mottl. But the official copyright register lists at least six names for this musical and even Robert Stoltz is entitled to a share in the royalties for this most famous of all collaborative stage productions.

We noted that the death of Karl Millöcker in 1899 marks the end of the golden age of the Viennese operetta, and that the premiere of the *Merry Widow* in 1905 marks the beginning of the next era. But when this one ended has not been decided yet. Its most important masters were still composing when the sound film industry began, were still active in the 1950s, and continued to write operettas after that time—they have not been long forgotten. Where in former times theaters played operettas by Lehár, Kalmán, Straus, Fall, and Kreisler, they are now playing imported musicals originating in London or New York. Theater managements continue to promise that in the foreseeable future there will also be a Viennese answer to the American musical, but we have not heard it yet. We must be patient. There have always been intermissions, even in the history of the City of Music.

The Musical Present

What is generally called music history reaches as far as Anton von Webern's death, history that can be rewritten and reinterpreted. But from there on we are more or less in the present, which a book on the City of Music, Vienna, can not afford to overlook. There must be musicians who were born in Vienna in this century, or who moved to Vienna, or were more or less permanent guests there. Otherwise the great development that began sometime in the past and which Schönberg predicted and guaranteed would last another hundred years after 1922, would suddenly have been interrupted and finished.

It is, however, very difficult to write about the present or the immediate past. One easily forgets what does not fit into one's personal musical world image. Perhaps one sees one's contemporaries and their work in a completely wrong light. Should I therefore refer in these last few pages to official membership lists of musical organizations, or undeniable successes in the world at large? That would be the cheapest method, and so I will not use it.

I would rather approach this subject from a very personal and therefore more vulnerable point of view, using methods for which I apologize in advance, both to the people about whom I write and to the public at large. We are fast approaching the end of the 20th century, and therefore have every chance, if things are progressing normally, of proving that Vienna is a City of Music, and that this is manifested for a third time. At least the preconditions are still there.

When Arnold Schönberg found his first important students, some composers made music in Vienna who either did not want to join his revolution or could not. This is to say that there were composers of opera of the caliber and success of Erich Wolfgang Korngold or, later, Franz Schmidt. Korngold was the son of the then music critic of the *Neue Freie Presse*. For half his lifetime he had to put up with the accusations of his avant garde contemporaries that he benefited from his father's protection and influence. They were annoyed by the fact that his works, like the opera *The Dead City* (Die Tote Stadt) became an undisputed public success. Schmidt came from Pressburg (Bratislava) to Vienna, and was a member of the Vienna Philharmonic. Despite the success of his opera *Notre Dame* and his thrilling oratorio *The Book of Seven Seals*, his reputation suffered some damage because he, like many musicians in Vienna, allegedly did not vigorously reject the tenets of National Socialism.

Korngold was a very successful opera composer. He not only attained his success as a composing child prodigy, but even as a mature man retained the respect of musicians. After his forced emigration to America he knew what to compose there and received various prizes for his film scores. After 1945 he tentatively returned to his native city and might have settled down again in his homeland. But the times were not favorable, and only after he had died did some of his music become successful in Vienna and elsewhere, the success which for a composer of operas is the only one that counts: the success with the public that likes to hear operas and applauds spontaneously at the important moments.

Franz Schmidt had a staunch following in Vienna. Tribute was paid him not only locally but also beyond the national frontiers. The Vienna Philharmonic Orchestra remained faithful to their former colleague. It can also be said that in several of his com-

Erich Wolfgang Korngold, son of a Viennese music critic, suffered, when he was still a child prodigy, from the fact that his father was a staunch conservative. The progressive Viennese—from Karl Kraus to Ernst Krenek—declared that his success was entirely due to his father. They could not have anticipated, though, that his opera "Die Tote Stadt" (The Dead City) would still be produced today with considerable success.

positions he had found his own idiom that musicians in all the world can understand and appreciate. Much musical refinement is contained in the entr'acte music for *Notre Dame*, and the oratorio based on the Book of Revelation is indeed grandiose. It is one of the few recent contributions to the art of oratorio. His *Book of the Seven Seals* is still effective today as the work of a master of composition showing unique musical inspiration.

"Between two fronts" is probably not the label that an Austrian composer like Egon Wellesz would have appreciated. Yet he grew up in Vienna, a pupil and serious advocate of progress, which meant of Arnold Schönberg. He was very successful as a musicologist and composer and was a founding member of an international music society that has become world-famous. He was chased out of town by National Socialism and settled in England where he became an active scholar but remained silent as a composer. It was indeed fortunate that after the war Egon Wellesz chose to write music again, and that in surroundings that reminded him of his native country. Some of his symphonies have, as yet, not been fully appreciated in all their beauty, but they do belong in the great Viennese tradition and will be one day understood as such. Wellesz returned to his home town only as a guest, though always as a former Viennese. He was honored in England and is almost always called a British composer. Vienna still has to make him one of hers.

Ernst Krenek, born in 1900, and before the Second World War one of the internationally famous Viennese musicians, has since become an American citizen. His wonderful opera *Jonny spielt auf* (Johnny Strikes Up, 1927) was played throughout Europe. He

ᛋᛋ Wiener und Wienerinnen! ᛋᛋ

Die Zersetzung und Vergiftung unserer bodenständigen Bevölkerung durch das östliche Gesindel nimmt einen gefahrdrohenden Umfang an. Nicht genug, daß unser Volk durch die Geldentwertung einer durchgreifenden Ausplünderung zugeführt wurde, sollen nun auch alle sittlich-kulturellen Grundfesten unseres Volkstumes zerstört werden.

Unsere Staatsoper,

die erste Kunst- und Bildungsstätte der Welt, der Stolz aller Wiener,

ist einer frechen jüdisch-negerischen Besudelung zum Opfer gefallen.

Das Schandwerk eines tschechischen Halbjuden

„Jonny spielt auf!"

in welchem Volk und Heimat, Sitte, Moral und Kultur brutal zertreten werden soll, wurde der Staatsoper aufgezwungen. Eine volksfremde Meute von Geschäftsjuden und Freimaurern setzt alles daran, unsere Staatsoper zu einer Bedürfnisanstalt ihrer jüdisch-negerischen Perversitäten herabzuwürdigen. Der Kunst-Bolschewismus erhebt frech sein Haupt. Die Schamröte muß jedem anständigen Wiener ins Gesicht steigen, wenn er hört, welch ungeheuerliche Schmach und Demütigung der berühmten Musikstadt Wien durch volksfremdes Gesindel angetan wurde

Da die christlich-großdeutsche Regierung diesem schamlosen Treiben untätig zusieht und von keiner Seite eine Abwehr versucht wird, so rufen wir alle Wiener zu einer

Riesen-
Protest-Kundgebung

auf, in welcher über die Wahrheit der jüdischen Verseuchung unseres Kunstlebens und über die der Staatsoper angetane Schmach gesprochen werden wird.

Christliche Wiener und Wienerinnen, Künstler, Musiker, Sänger und Antisemiten erscheint in Massen und protestiert mit uns gegen diese unerhörten Schandzustände in Oesterreich.

Ort: Lembachers Saal, Wien, III., Landstraße Hauptstraße.

Zeitpunkt: Freitag, den 13. Jänner 1928, 8 Uhr abends.

Kostenbeitrag: 20 Groschen. / Juden haben keinen Zutritt!

Nationalsozialistische deutsche Arbeiterpartei
Großdeutschlands.

Long before the annexation of Austria, Vienna learned how National Socialism reacted to modern music. In 1928 Ernst Krenek's opera Jonny spielt auf (Johnny Strikes Up) provided an excuse for an antisemitic demonstration. Ten years later the Viennese were still amazed at how such a thing could have happened. They had not taken the swastika seriously enough.

then decided to employ Schönberg's twelve-tone technique and wrote *Charles the Fifth* in this mode. For 50 years he had to bear the great disappointment that the Vienna State Opera had accepted this work in 1933 but did not perform it until 1984. Krenek emigrated to the U.S.A. and was active as a teacher and writer for half a century. He fully measured up to the young musicians who after Webern composed in a "serial" manner and was one of the earlier composers to try to make modern electronics useful in composition. But he fell in with "tendencies" and "innovations" only to the extent that he felt them to be progressive and able to enrich the musical tradition. His late works do not sound resigned but again very European, Austrian, and old Viennese in a non-folkloristic sense. Of him we must report that Vienna remembered him very late, but not too late, and that he maintained many connections with the City even in his old age, though he never returned. He clearly understood the honor bestowed when the Viennese proudly proclaimed him as one of their famous composers.

Completely removed from the trends described so far stands the Austrian composer Theodor Berger. Born in 1905 he was a world-wide traveller who finally settled in Vienna, nearly forgotten and unknown there. His compositions have been played by the Vienna Philharmonic under its leading conductors and were immediate public successes. But this success, at a time when a very young and curious generation had no successes to which to compare his work, deprived Berger of the recognition due him. It is quite possible that this situation might change and that he and his solid way of music making might some day be appreciated.

At present Gottfried von Einem almost holds the status of an official composer. At the Salzburg Festival his opera *Danton's Death* earned a resounding success that was never quite repeated. Gradually, but with full awareness, he took on the role of conservator and, even more, that of anti-avant-gardist. Von Einem's works are presented on many opera stages; he is equally and instantly successful with his orchestral works. Recently his string quartets have become favorites of young Viennese musicians.

His natural counterpart, though he never presented himself to the world as such, is Friedrich Cerha, an older representative of the young generation, so to speak. In Vienna he took on the role of pioneer and has, as an active musician, become an advocate for all the music that has been written or experimented with since Webern. He is characterized by strictness and seriousness, and possesses a quality that can perhaps be described as a sense of responsibility. He was convinced that, after Schönberg and Webern, composers could no longer make music as before. With his first grand opera *Baal* (after Bert Brecht) he seemed to imply that one has to compose like Alban Berg. Cerha is a Viennese of a special brand, although one would not necessarily conclude so on superficial acquaintance. He even tried, in his way, to compose something typically Viennese: his *Keintate* which was immediately successful. There is no doubt that he must be numbered among the important musicians of today.

But wherever this sort of speculation begins, naming of names must end, for the composers under 50 living in Vienna who also speak of Vienna in their compositions are numerous. We hope that they find understanding in the world around them, and also with future generations whose verdict cannot be anticipated here. To put it in simple terms: They still have time in their favor.

Great Musicians as Guests in Vienna

In this little book we have so far defined Viennese composers as those who were either born in Vienna or lived here for a good part of their lives. The city owes them its reputation as the City of Music and it is they who shaped our history.

Yet we must not ignore the fact that at all times illustrious guests frequented the city, either for short visits that gave them a taste of its special flavor that they, in turn, passed on to the world at large, or they composed something during their brief "guest appearance" in Vienna, thus contributing directly and actively to the musical history of the city. A concise and necessarily incomplete chapter may recall some of the most important of these visitors. The reader may be surprised whom the author, who is a local patriot, calls merely a "guest."

Antonio Vivaldi, born in Venice in 1678, extraordinarily famous in his time as a composer and as "il prete rosso" (the red-haired priest), was a Venetian composer who had written a good deal of instrumental music before he turned to opera. When his reputation had spread far beyond Italy and he was invited by German princely courts, he passed through Vienna, for the first time in 1729/30, when the city was a great center of Italian opera. In 1740 he came once more from Italy, which was his last visit to the imperial city. He wanted to serve at the Imperial Court and hoped for a renewal of his reputation that in Venice had suffered, both at the human and musical level, a noticeable and painful setback. He did make music in Vienna, but did not manage to revive his fame of old: The Emperor who had invited him, Charles VI, died just before Vivaldi arrived, and the "Most Reverend Father, Antonnj Vivaldi, secular priest", (this was the entry in the registry of deaths of St. Stephen's) only lived another six months before he died in poverty, on July 28, 1741, and was buried in the now gone cemetery near the Church of St. Charles. The world still admires Antonio Vivaldi's concertos, but does not remember that Vienna was the composer's last abode. Vivaldi was and remained a guest.

Much longer and more consequential was the stay in Vienna of Christoph Willibald von Gluck (1714–1787), the great reformer of opera. He had been active in Vienna as a chamber musician before settling for good in 1752. In 1774 he became "Court Compositeur", thus obtaining a steady employment and commissions to compose operas and ballets. All works that were later regarded as his greatest, were written for Vienna. Many of his operas whose titles are hardly known today had their first performances in this city. Yet I must admit without envy that Gluck belonged to the world at large, possessing none of the characteristics of a Viennese composer. *Orpheus and Eurydice* was first performed at the Court Theatre in 1762; the encyclopedias note that this performance was as important as the Paris version of 1772. One hundred repeat performances are known to have taken place in Vienna, and we also know of the special enthusiasm of the Empress Maria Theresia for this work. Yet the great dispute over the nature of "opera" did not take place in Vienna but in Paris where the admirers of Gluck and those of Piccini fended. Consequently Gluck wrote his two *Iphigenia* operas for Paris.

To continue with the term "guest in our town:" Gioacchino Rossini (1792–1868) was certainly not a Viennese composer. Yet he managed to provoke an enthusiasm that was part of the customary craze over "Italianitá." He was admired by Beethoven and was responsible for the composition of the "Italian Overture" which Franz Schubert wrote in order to prove to his friends that one doesn't have to be born in Pesaro to produce a brilliant masterpiece.

There are dozens of stories about the Rossini fever that broke out in Vienna. That the maestro considered himself a representative of the Italian Opera singers, thus competing with the native forces, and not at all a Viennese composer, must come as no surprise. In just the same way the licencees of Vienna theaters preferred to make money by catering to the Italian tastes of the local nobility, thus delaying for years the popularity of German opera. Their great supplier of operas, Rossini, always remaining a stranger to the city.

Carl Maria von Weber (1786–1826), the epitome of German Romanticism, has a better claim to have his close ties to Vienna pointed out here: His uncle was the father-in-law of Wolfgang Amadeus Mozart and he himself studied music with Michael Haydn in Salzburg and later with Abbé Vogler. This influential theatrical producer—Weber was not only composer, but, on the side, what today would be called a theatrical producer—wrote his penultimate opera for the Kärntnertor Theater. This was *Euryanthe* which was premiered there in 1823 and of which at least the overture can still be heard today. It is so charming that one could imagine the whole opera might be worth producing, were it not for the completely baffling libretto by a woman writer, Helmina von Chézy. Weber lived in Vienna, but always like a travelling theater impresario and under constant pressure to make money. He did not live very well in our town.

Frédéric Chopin (1810–1849), during his first visit in 1829 to Vienna, hoping to place some of his compositions with a Viennese music publisher, heard some operas by Rossini and was received by the musical public with enthusiasm. How else could we explain that having arrived in early August of 1829 he could, by the end of the month, take part in a "Musical Academy" (a concert) at which, after a Beethoven overture, two of his own compositions were performed? "My free improvisation was nothing to brag about, but there was even more applause" he wrote, satisfied with the Viennese public. Soon after his first visit he composed some waltzes. But he was not a grateful musician: Though

Christoph Willibald Gluck managed to cause more sensation and discussion in Paris than in Vienna by virtue of his operatic reforms. His faithful friends Haydn and, above all, Salieri, and later Beethoven and Schubert, both Salieri's students, were all familiar with and supportive of his ideas.

Gioacchino Rossini, here shown after an etching by August Weger, was very fond of Vienna, the city where, before him, his adored Mozart had lived. His operas were fêted there as elsewhere and the Viennese made him a hero. Schubert, sure of his own capabilities, composed his Overture in the Italian Style, *simply to prove that he could write the same kind of music.*

in December of 1830 he returned for a long visit and was lionized by society, his mind was only on money and his success as a composer and virtuoso. In the course of his visit he made this snide remark: "The most popular Viennese entertainments are evenings in local taverns where Strauss and Lanner (they are the local Swiescewscys) play waltzes for the diners. There is tremendous applause after each waltz, and when they play a "quodlibet", i.e., a medley of melodies from operas, songs and dances, the listeners are so enthusiastic that they do not know what to do. That proves the spoiled taste of the Viennese." This spoiled public was quite ready to applaud him too, but Chopin never became a Viennese composer.

Hector Berlioz (1803–1869) was certainly no Viennese, but rightly went down in history as *The* Parisian composer. But we can make some claim on him as a lover of Vienna. He admitted that he was an admirer of Johann Strauss, the Elder, and later transferred his admiration and loyalty to Johann Strauss, Junior, the Waltz King. His numerous concert tours also took him to Vienna, where he was popular not only among the orchestra members but the audience as well. Budapest was really more important to him,

Vienna, the City of Music, was, of course, the goal of all travelling virtuosos who excited frenzies of applause in all of Europe. Nicolò Paganini, the legendary "devil's violinist," who managed to keep this reputation to this very day, also performed in Vienna, as did, after him, Franz Liszt, whose concerts caused a sensation in Viennese society. But such events led only to a few anecdotes and nostalgic reminiscences of great concert evenings.

and for a performance of his own compositions in Hungary he even borrowed the "Rákóczy March." The waltz included in his *Symphonie Fantastique* can hardly be interpreted as an homage to Vienna, for the "grand ball" that Berlioz was depicting simply demanded a waltz.

And what about Franz Liszt (1811–1886)? Well, although he was a Hungarian musician and should have had some affinities to the capital of the Empire in which he was born, he was drawn to the world outside. He was more at home in Germany and Rome than in Vienna where his type of music was never very popular. We may remember that Vienna was the city of Eduard Hanslick and Johannes Brahms, and that though the public rallied enthusiastically to the rare guest performances of the pianist Liszt, as audiences did everywhere in the world, and though Johann Strauss, Junior even gave a musical soirée in honor of the composer, Liszt's music, in the last analysis, never took root. We can easily comprehend why Liszt came back several times: Vienna was a recognized capital of Music and a virtuoso of his rank simply *had* to be successful there. Even a Liszt could not afford to ignore the City altogether.

Richard Wagner's relationship to Vienna was ambivalent. He was thrilled by the performances of his Tannhäuser *and* Lohengrin *and had high praise for the Opera House. But when his* Tristan *was not premiered there after many rehearsals, he thought in a different way about the Viennese musical world. (Drawing by Gustav Gaul)*

Richard Wagner (1813–1883) is quite a different story. He had, as is probably well known, a real chance of becoming a Viennese composer. Or didn't he? To be accurate, Vienna was for Wagner the last stepping stone on the road to real recognition, before being called to Munich by Ludwig II of Bavaria in 1864. In Vienna the composer was still waiting, ready for the jump into fame; he wrote and theorized, and found a particularly understanding milliner who sewed his wardrobe, not only during his time in Vienna, but for many years, thus gaining entry into the history of music. Yet despite some contacts with Viennese composers, among them Brahms, and despite many Viennese admirers who recognized his greatness, Wagner did not really feel at home in Vienna. He was a German composer through and through. As far as the milliner is concerned, Wagner's letters to her have been preserved, and were, with Brahms' help, played into the hands of a very active anti-Wagnerian, the journalist Daniel Spitzer, who published them, not increasing Wagner's fondness for Vienna. The cultivation of Wagner's works in Vienna has its own respectable history. We know of the many successful, and painful, attempts by Wagner to have *Tristan und Isolde* premiered at the Vienna Court Opera. But it is hardly known that the Vienna Men's Choir had rehearsed all Wagner choruses and was performing them in public before they had been heard on stage. Nor that Johann Strauss' band at their concerts played potpourris from Wagner's operas with great success—which shows that the Vienna public was ready for innovations. The continuing streams of Viennese Wagner fans making their pilgrimage to Bayreuth suggest a revision of the notion of Vienna's anti-Wagnerian attitude is in order. And did not Anton Bruckner, whom we may call one of the most touching Wagnerites, live in Vienna? And was not Hugo Wolf, the great Lieder composer, an outspoken admirer of Wagner?

Hugo Wolf (1860–1903) has to be mentioned here as well, as a composer who loved Vienna. He studied for three years at the Vienna Conservatory of the Friends of Music Society, and being the frequent guest of a Viennese family of jewelers he was practically a Viennese himself. For four years he wrote the most biting and vicious musical critiques that have ever appeared in Vienna. And his end was in tragically Viennese style: He succumbed to "mental obscuration," as they used to say politely in those days. Soon after Gustav Mahler had been named Director of the Court Opera, Wolf ran through the streets of Vienna, yelling that *he* was the new director of the Opera.

Not a word about his more than 310 Lieder? About his wonderful chamber music, his *Feuerreiter* (fire rider) and his opera *The Corregidor*? Well, as Viennese as Schubert's songs are, as completely without any local affinity are the great songs of Hugo Wolf. Rather they follow Robert Schumann and, today, are the property of the entire world. The musician Hugo Wolf, whom we love and admire, has, on the one hand, lived and suffered in Vienna, but is, on the other, anything but a Viennese composer.

One could identify many more composers who, in one way or another, are claimed by Vienna as theirs, but cannot, on closer investigation, be called Viennese. Just to quote

After World War I Richard Strauss became Director of the Vienna State Opera, against the wishes of his text writer, Hugo von Hofmannsthal. He did, however, his most successful premieres in Dresden. He composed his Die Frau ohne Schatten (The Woman without a Shadow) and the ballet Schlagobers (Whipped Cream) for Vienna. This sketch by W. Bithorn shows Hofmannsthal and Strauss in close collaboration.

an example from our days: The Hungarian György Ligeti has his official residence in Vienna, is an Austrian citizen, has friends in town and is an outspoken admirer of Schubert. He is an internationally known master and could easily be "at home" in any other city. He does, in fact, reside for very short periods in his Vienna apartment, and has no objection to being counted euphemistically among the Viennese composers, although he knows only too well that he is not a Viennese composer.

Much the same can be said of Roman Haubenstock-Ramati who hails from Poland, once made Paris his home, and is now Professor of Composition in Vienna. He is much too international in his music to be called a Viennese, yet he has a Viennese lifestyle. He is a frequent visitor to the Viennese coffee houses and is often seen in Viennese society where he has taken up a quiet but respected place. But he himself would be astonished if we insisted on calling him a Viennese composer.

Then there is Leonard Bernstein who lives and composes elsewhere but loves to make music with the Vienna Philharmonic. We might rather call him a Viennese in disguise in his overall attitude, and he would not mind our doing so.

This is about as far as we can go in our enumeration, written to prove that Vienna is a City of Music which harbors both real Viennese composers and those who practice their profession as guests. At any rate: This chapter was necessary to round our little account of music in Vienna.

The Vienna State Opera

It is really impossible to say how old this institution is. Consequently even in Vienna, where one is very conscious of tradition, one celebrates only the anniversaries of the building—the one that today is called the Opera House on the Ring. In reality, the foundation of the Vienna Opera may safely be placed in the Baroque era, when, with the lively participation of the Imperial family, operas were performed not only for the aristocracy on special occasions, but for the whole population on a regular basis. Out of the ensembles that were, at that time, rapidly succeeding each other and yet received the characteristic imprints of various Court Kapellmeister or Court Composers, there developed what we call today the Vienna State Opera, almost like a cultural toy, watched, loved, and criticized by everyone.

We shall not go far back into the past, and only mention that at least as late as Mozart the Italian opera caused a sensation under the auspices of Antonio Salieri, and that German light opera or *Singspiel* made its debut here. At the time of Beethoven the suburban theatres in Vienna, like the Theater an der Wien that still exists today, became well-known for their exquisite performances of operas, aside from the Imperial Opera House, and premiered such works as *Fidelio*. Let us not forget that during the 19th century when Carl Maria von Weber was in Vienna and Conradin Kreutzer was "Opernchef" (Director of the Opera) the programs consisted chiefly of works by contemporary composers, unlike today's usual repertory of "museum pieces."

When in the last third of the past century the great expansion of the city took place, the Ring boulevard was created and the magnificent structures went up that are today regarded as the homes of traditional artistic culture. One of these is the Court Opera and only two small details of its history need be noted here.

First, a remark on the tragic fate of the two architects, one of whom committed suicide because of harsh criticisms while the other died soon after of a "broken heart" as was said at the time. The underlying cause is the relatively high elevation of the Ring when it was completed, causing the building to appear as if it had sunk into the ground, which had not been foreseen when construction was begun. Public criticism was shared by the Emperor and, according to rumor, a critical remark of the Emperor was the immediate cause of the suicide. After that incident the Emperor never again offered any criticism in public.

The other point that is of historic interest here is the fact that Eduard Hanslick, member of a specially appointed committee and a purported enemy of Richard Wagner, insisted on having the latter's name included in the memorial gallery of famous opera composers. The opponent of the composer still recognized the true greatness of this master and was fair enough to have his name included among those honored.

The Imperial Opera House was run, until the end of the monarchy, as the personal responsibility of the Emperor, that is to say, the moneys necessary for its operation were provided by the imperial household, the artistic director being responsible to an imperial administrator. Consequently, though hardly ever mentioned, every visitor, Viennese or foreign, could consider himself a guest of His Majesty.

Great artists have, for centuries, made unusual efforts to become artistic director of the Opera House. Gustav Mahler forwent his Jewish religious affiliation in order to be

The New Kärntnertor Theater stood just inside the old city walls, not far from the spot where today one can see the Vienna State Opera. It was the second "firm" (i.e. brick-built) theater built by the Habsburgs. As the center of great performances of ballet and Italian and German operas, it was the scene of many great contests between Italian and German opera, and as such the direct forerunner of today's great opera house.

able to become musical director of the house. Richard Strauss put up with Franz Schalk as co-director in order to be the Director of the State Opera. Karl Böhm, during World War II, dropped the Dresden Opera appointment to accept a call to Vienna, and Herbert von Karajan organized several concert performances of operas at the Vienna *Musikverein* in order to make it known that he was interested in this position which was soon after offered to him.

The importance of this institution in Vienna is most likely best illustrated by the fact that even in 1918, at the height of financial crises, there was no discussion about raising the funds necessary to keep the Opera House open. To this day, there has never been any doubt that Vienna *must* have an Opera House of international fame, comparable to institutions in far larger and richer countries.

After World War II, during the last few days of which the Opera House on the Ring was destroyed, it was not only a foregone conclusion that the Vienna Opera had to be re-built in all its former glory, but a highly important decision of cultural policy also was made. Austria sought good will and political recognition in Belgium, France and London by staging there performances by the entire company. These artistic and political objectives were accomplished.

A whole garland of stories is woven around the history of the Vienna Opera, most of which contain a kernel of truth. It is a matter of fact that almost all the great composers of all periods were proud to be able to write for it, or at least tried to be successful there. Indeed, the Vienna Opera was always a synonym for conservative recognition and glory.

The most important opera composers had been drawn to this institution for centuries, for a success here carried a stamp of approval of which any composer would be proud.

As long as this was the case, the Vienna Opera possessed an ensemble whose leading singers were in demand for guest appearances all over the world. Though there have been basic changes in opera life, guest appearances in Vienna by the great conductors or interpreters continue to carry great prestige.

As long as this situation continued many operas received first performances in Vienna, even though admittedly only a few could be classified as lasting successes, especially in the 20th century. Since the commissioning of operas has become customary again, the Vienna Opera has remained modestly in the background and contributed relatively little to a rejuvenation of the opera repertoire.

Of the oft-repeated stories, that every Viennese would like to be the director of the State Opera and that every man in the street knows all there is to know about the singers and performances, barely half can be said to be true. But even that tells us something important about the significance of the institution. Discussions about the future of the Vienna State Opera do indeed draw the attention of a very wide circle of the population. Conversations about a past or future director of the opera are common not only among opera enthusiasts but can be heard in Parliament or on the street. One reason for this is the enormous financial outlay of public funds required for high caliber opera. Furthermore, the high level of this institution is seen as indicative of the artistic standards of the whole country. Austrians, whether they are really interested in music or not, enjoy being regarded as the inhabitants of a music-loving country.

In our time, thanks to the televising and broadcasting of opera performances over the whole world, the genre has enjoyed increased popularity. It is no wonder that the Vienna Opera attaches great value to the reputation of being Vienna's central institution, and that the city is willing to concede this.

But the whole truth about the rank of the Vienna State Opera is much more complicated and can hardly be presented adequately in a short history like this. This institution over the years attracted a type of artist-worker who guarantees, in all circumstances, a fundamentally excellent performance: The orchestra, the chorus, the technical personnel of the Vienna Opera have gained a reputation throughout the world of being the best in the field. And that is one of the reasons why great stars who could easily obtain lucrative engagements in other opera houses singing any roles they desired, continue to come to Vienna.

While the Vienna public is perhaps not more expert than patrons elsewhere, they are both extremely stubborn and well informed. Even if one admits that the Italians understand more about voice quality than other opera lovers, and even if one knows that in Germany some daring new opera production would have more success than elsewhere, one still has to admit that the Vienna Opera public has an exceptionally good memory. Even after some years it is still ready to applaud profusely and lovingly a conductor or singer to remind him or her and themselves that once he or she was outstandingly good. In Vienna they call this loyalty and hardly give it another thought, but the musical friend from abroad may need such an explanation. Here a single opera performance is hardly ever judged as such, either positively or negatively, but, as is customary in a family, by the total of the artist's past achievements.

In a time that has become rather insensitive, in which even artists have learned how to handle flight tickets, schedules and income tax demands, the Vienna Opera has, like all important opera houses, retained something of a character that can hardly be expressed in figures, something that still attracts opera lovers, both passive and active ones alike, and is not likely to disappear in the future.

That the State Opera takes its whole ensemble, including large productions, on tour is part and parcel of the institution. In Japan, for instance, a very important "market" exists for records and, in general, for western culture. An artist, a whole orchestra or even a whole opera company that wants to maintain its reputation, must make guest appearances. Tours in the USA and in the Soviet Union are likewise part of the cultural and political concept and therefore not neglected.

During the summer months, however, the Vienna music lover may be allowed to move away from his native city and go to Salzburg. The summer festival there offers its own productions that can only be seen there, but the forces at work there are largely those to be seen and heard during the season in Vienna. One can in good faith recommend that a guest from abroad who comes to Austria during the summer attend a performance at Salzburg, where the Vienna Opera goes on vacation, so to speak. This may be an overstatement if examined in detail, but it is correct in general. One can prove this by simply pointing out that all attempts at giving summer opera in Vienna and also promoting the Salzburg Festival have failed, because they are mutually exclusive. The Salzburg Festival has to close the day before the season in Vienna begins.

The Vienna Philharmonic

Before we turn to one or the other of the Viennese orchestras it is necessary to remind the reader that the history of orchestras as we hear them today on the concert stages of the world is not that old. They were unknown before the middle class developed an interest in this form of music. Even around 1800, when a considerable amount of music that we appreciate today had already been composed, only small orchestras, so-called "Kapellen", composed of professional musicians in the service of a local prince or high church dignitary existed. For the very rare public performances, as we think of them today, by one of these orchestras, a larger ensemble would be created by adding other musicians. There are many accounts of public performances in Vienna in which a large orchestra, such as we know it today, was augmented by a number of important composers who participated out of friendship and appreciation for their composer-colleague at the first stand, irrespective of whether this was their usual place or not.

Only with the growth of what is generally called bourgeois musical culture in the best sense of the word, did real orchestras develop. The best known of these had more or less the same history: They were formed one day out of the core of an existing "Kapelle" for the purpose of making music together and deriving a livelihood from it.

This then was also the origin of the Vienna Philharmonic, when they and their conductor, Otto Nicolai, wanted to be heard not just as an opera orchestra, but also as a concert orchestra. Nicolai was not a Viennese. Born in Königsberg, North Germany, in 1810, he worked in Vienna as a composer and conductor for only two brief periods in his life: Once as an opera conductor under Conradin Kreutzer during the season of 1837/38 and then as a Court Kapellmeister from 1841 to 1847. Yet he is generally regarded as the founder of the ensemble which has since become a most typical Viennese institution, and which has remained faithful to his legacy through the generations. To this day, one of the subscription concerts is specifically named "Nicolai" concert, and is for all connoisseurs at least a very significant concert by virtue of the conductor who is chosen to conduct it.

And what about the orchestra itself? Well, the very special structure of the Vienna Philharmonic has given it an advantage among most other great orchestras. They are an independent private corporation, so by law run their affairs unconstrained by the wishes of outsiders. For all practical purposes, however, the orchestra has never been managed in quite this way. The orchestra has always consisted of members of the Vienna Opera Orchestra, now known as the State Opera. It was therefore closely tied to whoever was the latter's director or first conductor, and consequently the person filling this role was always chosen with great care as they set the tone at the Court Opera as well as of the Philharmonic concerts.

For many years this position bore the mark of a conductor-in-chief. Once the conductor was chosen by the orchestra, he conducted almost all their concerts and was responsible for choosing their programs. Only when in the course of the 20th century musical life tended toward versatility and brilliance of performance, did the Vienna Philharmonic cease binding itself exclusively to a single musical director, but invited important guest conductors as well. During the years between the wars this practice developed into a kind of sport. Today's Vienna Philharmonic is well known for the fact that in these times of fierce competition for a famous principal conductor, all possible candidates have frequently appeared as guest conductors.

It would be senseless to list all the permanent conductors of former years: The great ones, like Hans von Bülow and Hans Richter, and the important ones, like Felix von Weingartner and Franz Schalk, but also the conducting composers like Gustav Mahler and Richard Strauss were among them. There are numerous anecdotes about them and the orchestra; they are all preserved and repeated by word of mouth and also set down in print in testimonial books. Here let it be noted that some of the most famous conductors did not feel at home with the orchestra, but could not resist an invitation from the orchestra. And with some pride one observes what an independent personality the orchestra itself has.

In order to comprehend this strange state of affairs, the reader has to call to mind what it means to be an active participant in the Music Capital, Vienna, to be a member of the Vienna Philharmonic. First of all, he is a life member of the Vienna Opera and as such a respected civil servant. Secondly, he has, once appointed by his elder colleagues as a member of the private club that the Vienna Philharmonic is, achieved great musical recognition. Lastly, he becomes, as a rule, a member of at least one of the fine chamber music groups—countless quartets and other ensembles—staffed exclusively by members of the Vienna Philharmonic. Thanks to clever scheduling all these ensembles can perform, tour and continue to participate in the orchestra concerts. Finally, a member of the Vienna Philharmonic is, in most cases, an instructor at the State Academy of Music or at the Conservatory and in this way, too, concerned with the training of a new generation of musicians in the city.

As humble as the position of "musician" was in the past, it is an honorable one in Vienna now and has been so for many generations. Whatever honors and decorations or public recognition can come to a musician, a member of the Vienna Philharmonic is most likely to receive them. Nobody questions why this is so in today's society. The public has become used to it and are proud to keep it that way.

Members of the Vienna Philharmonic, when asked about the particular characteristics of the orchestra, always mention two outstanding conductors who have, on special occasions, made speeches about them: Wilhelm Furtwängler and Karl Böhm. The gist of the speeches was that the special attraction of the way the Vienna Philharmonic play, lay in the fact that they had all been products of the same school. This does not imply a narrow, parochial idea of "school" and, certainly not reducing it to a single locality, as is easily done. The Vienna Philharmonic has always attracted leading members who were not born in Vienna. They hailed from areas that traditionally furnished players to Vienna and still do so today. In fact, there are brass players from Vienna but also from Czechoslovakia, and string players from all the countries that formerly formed the Empire. From one decade to another one would have to take into account different areas, other villages which still exist.

And, of course, there are some "Philharmonic family names" which can be traced back in the history of the orchestra to 1900, active musicians in the third generation in the orchestra who, in some instances, have inherited the instruments they are playing from their grandfathers or in other cases who have changed to another instrument. That 1938 was the year in which the Jewish membership of the orchestra was wiped out is part of the history of the institution that must not ever be lost sight of. None of those who emigrated to make music in the U.S.A. returned after the war. But every one of them is touched when reminded of the fact that he was once a member of the orchestra.

It would be going too far to reproach the institution with any kind of prejudice. Yet, it continues to be the only large orchestra which includes no women. After many public debates, that often turned into noisy scenes, it was calmly decided to remain an all-male ensemble for as long as possible. As a private corporation the Vienna Philharmonic has no obligation to respond to public criticism of this or any other matter if it chooses not to do so. Women are allowed to audition but the winner is always a male candidate. The great wave of women's liberation seems to have made this matter topical. But the debates are over, and while all other Viennese orchestras have changed policy and admitted women, the Vienna Philharmonic play without them.

The Philharmonic plays relatively rarely in Vienna. It is required to play the scheduled evenings at the Opera and perform a meagre dozen concerts of their own, always on Saturday afternoon and Sunday morning. The consequence is that it does not appoint more than ten conductors per season and that its repertoire has remained relatively limited. The "avant-garde" therefore call them extremely conservative, and the orchestra long ago gave up any effort to counter them. In their long history they have given many first performances that have caused sensations. They also are acquainted with the latest trends in music, for many of their members play in other ensembles that perform modern music exclusively. In their concerts, however, they play only the classical repertoire or, in agreement with their conductors who are interested in doing so, some rarities from other periods of music. On the great concert tours that they undertake annually they usually stick, for good reasons, to classical Viennese music. Our musical friends from around the world who can afford the expense of attending a Vienna Philharmonic concert do not want, as a rule, to hear French or Russian music, but Haydn, Mozart, Beethoven, Schubert, and so on. And the orchestra has wisely decided to serve such wishes, thus being assured of success.

Every major orchestra is an assembly of highly distinct soloists. In the Philharmonic, the sum total of all these individually very different temperaments finds its common character at their plenary sessions when they generally agree on the following season's conductors and programs. As musicians they attach great value to self-discipline. They understand that they must live up to a world-wide reputation and are therefore prepared to work very hard to support it. It is important to them that their violins have their own special sound, achieved in many rehearsals. It is equally important to them that their solo wind players perform up to the famous "Philharmonic" standard.

Today's situation is such that tickets for the Philharmonic subscription concerts are not generally available for sale to the public. The ownership of a season ticket is a status symbol and the members of the Philharmonic Orchestra do everything in their power to keep it that way. They have learned from their history that during the inter-war years their concerts were seldom sold out, and that Arturo Toscanini, for example, was asked to conduct not only because of his musicianship but also thanks to his special attraction for the knowledgeable public. The main hall of the *Musikverein* has only slightly over 2000 seats. Given two performances of each program this means that less than 5000 music lovers are in a position to hear a program of their "native" orchestra.

And yet, those who claim to know the orchestra like their own family have some grounds for this assertion: it is the result of the many means of music reproduction available in our time. Many television and radio programs, and more recently filmed concerts and video cassettes, extend the options for the Vienna Philharmonic to remain popular and make a good living, an opportunity they do not wish to miss. Thus they retain all their potential for remaining the undisputed representative ensemble of the city.

The Vienna Symphonic Orchestra

On certain rare, official occasions the Vienna Symphonic Orchestra (Wiener Symphoniker) is called the Concert Orchestra of the City of Vienna. They are just that, and because of it they sometimes suffer from the fact that the Philharmonic manages to usurp a good deal of their international reputation.

This ensemble, which did not originally make music under this name, was founded in 1900 and has been the permanent concert orchestra of the city ever since. At least in recent times, the City of Vienna has been almost exclusively responsible for the orchestra and ensures its financial existence.

In contrast to their colleagues at the Opera the musicians of the Vienna Symphonic have to be on duty almost every night and very rarely have the opportunity to play under a conductor of their choice. They, too, function as a corporation, but they are rarely in a position to act as their own managers. That is to say, they are engaged by the two great concert institutions of the City and asked or ordered to collaborate with the musicians who have been engaged by the two institutions, and to play programs that fit into one or the other of the "cycles" of programs planned by the producers. The notion that the Vienna Symphonic Orchestra is always for hire is, of course, also untrue. The musicians have, for some time, been able to maintain a sort of voting right which is exercised, above all, in vetoing conductors or programs not to their liking. In truth, it is neither wise nor beneficial for a producer to force or constrain the Symphony Orchestra to put up with anybody or anything.

The orchestra which, during its history, has been led by some of the world's foremost conductors, has, during several periods in its immediate past, been very successful with several of its "principal conductors," either overtly holding that title or surreptitiously treated as such. For example, Herbert von Karajan, before he became the artistic director of the Vienna State Opera, was the dedicated conductor of the Vienna Symphonic, with whom he secretly plotted against the Vienna Philharmonic and his "rival" Wilhelm Furtwängler. A special "Karajan Series" with the Symphonic Orchestra was counted among the great musical events of the City. His "successor" who in fact became the chief conductor of the Symphonic Orchestra and for nearly 10 years helped to establish the character of the orchestra, was Wolfgang Sawallisch, who though young was soon allowed to choose his own series of concerts. Under Sawallisch, the orchestra undertook major tours to the U.S.A. and Japan, very conscious of its unique position.

Moreover, it was this orchestra which after World War II supplied the public with a badly needed update on the previously forbidden and unknown music of the previous decade. As there was, at that time, no Austrian radio orchestra in today's sense of the word, the Vienna Symphonic Orchestra took upon itself all those tasks that elsewhere were given to specialist ensembles. The entire musical literature of the 20th century was played and yet what is called in Vienna the "symphonic legacy" was not neglected. An active member of the Vienna Symphonic was, for many years, the best musical "all-rounder" to be found in Vienna. Moreover, he was a musician who, in the course of one season, became acquainted with numerous conductors.

Josef Krips, Carlo Maria Giulini, and Gennadi Roshdestvensky were among those who conducted the Symphonic Orchestra. Present international practice allows a few well-known conductors to hold at least two important positions simultaneously, with the consequence that they can not devote much time or sustained interest to either orchestra. The Symphonic Orchestra on the other hand deems it advisable to look for a single great musician who is willing to work with the orchestra throughout the year. Since the founding of the Bregenz Festival in western Austria the Vienna Symphonic has assumed the function of the festival orchestra. During the summer they also play for opera and operetta performances and have accepted, on special occasions, the function of an opera orchestra during the Vienna Festival Weeks. It was in this capacity that they played, in the Theater an der Wien, the premiere of Alban Berg's *Lulu,* Arnold Schönberg's *Expectation* and Mathias Hauer's *The Black Spider.*

And let it be noted that this orchestra has in its ranks as many soloists and members of small ensembles as their "competitors" have. It is, in fact, like every other large orchestra, a treasure trove for string quartets and other ensembles. The best known of these is most likely the "Concentus Musicus," the ensemble for old music, founded by the former member of the Symphonic, Nikolaus Harnoncourt, and led by him to world fame. The problems of organizing such ensembles in a way to guarantee a trouble-free working schedule for the whole orchestra are obviously enormous. And as everywhere else in the world, these difficulties can only be solved by friendly cooperation among colleagues. In addition many members of the Vienna Symphonic are respected professors and teachers, just as their colleagues from the Philharmonic.

In effect, the Viennese musicians in either of these large orchestras come out of the same "stable." Often only the fact that a vacancy opened at the right time in one or the other determined which orchestra a young musician would join. Only the expert can detect the slight differences there are with regard to prestige and salary. The demands made on the members of either orchestra and their wide field of experience are about equivalent. To be chosen a member of the Vienna Symphonic Orchestra means to be among the foremost ranks of orchestra musicians in a city that calls itself the City of Music.

Once More: The Court Chapel

We came to know them earlier: The *Hofmusikkapelle* that once was the army of musicians appointed and paid by the Emperor, so he could have music of the appropriate kind on all occasions that were important to him. This institution has lasted throughout the centuries and continues under the same name.

When the Monarchy on the Danube broke up at the end of World War I, the democratically elected representatives of the new republic, now a small country, agreed that this institution, consisting of instrumentalists and singers who assisted at the divine services for the Imperial family, was to be continued.

And so it still exists: Sunday after Sunday and, of course, on all church holidays, the music of the Hofmusikkapelle can be heard at the Imperial Court Chapel. Admission is by ticket only and intended mainly for guests from abroad who want to experience such a service. But there also remain certain groups within Viennese society who do not wish to forgo an "old-fashioned" Sunday service and who will regularly be found in attendance. The fundamental changes which, as some would have it, were not brought about by history or by the state, but by the Roman Catholic Church itself, left hardly any traces in the manner in which the Court Chapel makes music today. The Pope issued a decree specifically exempting Vienna and this chapel in particular from these various liturgical changes. Thus it is simpler in Vienna than elsewhere to perform the church compositions of the old (Renaissance) masters and those of Haydn, Mozart, Beethoven, Schubert and Bruckner that were written for ecclesiastical use.

They still observe the old church regulations and do not perform Masses with orchestra during Advent and Lent. On the Sundays when players must perform immediately after Mass in the Philharmonic Subscription Concerts, a shorter Mass is chosen. For in the Court Chapel the Vienna Choir Boys are engaged to sing the high solo parts, while the gentlemen of the State Opera Chorus sing the tenor and bass parts (outside professionals are occasionally engaged for solo parts). The members of the orchestra are, of course, all members of the Vienna Philharmonic.

An additional choir can also be heard in the Court Chapel, made up of former members of the Choir Boys, who, after their voices have changed, do not wish to forgo participating in choral singing. They do not sing as professionals, but under the name "Chorus Viennensis" and in church as "Schola Choralis." They chant the responses, offering the visitors a truly authentic sense of the richly decorative style of Roman Catholic church music services of former times.

The Court Chapel services are suspended during the summer months for the very simple reason that the members must be free in order either to participate in the Salzburg Festival or be on vacation. For the same reasons the Court Chapel is almost never on tour, so that its sound can only really be heard in the original setting and place. From the point of view of tourist promotion this is most likely a sad situation, but from a purely artistic point of view an ideal one as there is no booking beyond capacity and no mass production.

A final thought: The Court Chapel is still intact and pure and at the center of musical life in Vienna, despite the fact that few Viennese are aware of this.

The Vienna Choir Boys

When after World War II the Court Chapel resumed its services, they decided, first of all, to cut one expensive item and engage for soprano and alto parts the ladies of the State Opera Choir rather than maintain the specially trained members of the Boys Choir who always had received a general education as well, at government expense.

It was soon realized, however, that this was a possible, but certainly not an ideal solution. So a young priest who served in the Court Chapel began on his own initiative to look for boys' voices again. He spent his own private means to pay for their training and housing and most likely had nothing else in mind but to secure the boys' voices for the divine service. Had the times been more settled, he might have succeeded. But when he found himself in financial difficulties, he allowed the boys to appear in little "scenes" of secular music in Vienna which met with great success. This was the foundation of the "Vienna Choir Boys" which is today a very honorable private institution that guarantees that fully trained boys' voices are, at all times, ready for service in the Court Chapel.

The Vienna Choir Boys, whom even the Viennese usually think of as a publicly financed art institution like so many others, are proud to be self-supporting. They are paid an appropriate amount for their participation in the Court Chapel, as they are when they sing children's parts in the Vienna State Opera. And if there are other concerts where childrens' voices are needed, the Vienna Choir Boys are at their disposal for the usual fees—for oratorios, concert performances of Masses, for recording sessions.

But all this would not provide enough income to make it possible for the children to live in a boarding institution and receive the necessary training and musical schooling. The great tours that take place throughout the year in Europe, in the U.S.A. and in Japan, bring in the necessary means which under different circumstances and more usual Austrian practices would be supplied by the state.

It seems natural to them to be known as the "Singing Ambassadors of Austria," and that their performances of short operas and their interpretations of Viennese waltzes are more successful than their renderings of sacred music. But this is also a source of worry for the administration which is anxious to dispel any misconceptions about them. Guests from abroad have relatively few opportunities in Vienna to hear the Choir Boys. One may hear them at the services in the Court Chapel or attend one of their rare "at home" concerts in their residence, the Augarten Palace in Vienna.

That they do not appear constantly in public has its advantages for the boys who are, after all, normal children needing leisure time outside the limelight in which they must live while on tour.

The Society of Friends of Music (Gesellschaft der Musikfreunde) in Vienna

When speaking of the two great concert halls in Vienna, we simply use the shortened form: the Music Society (*Musikverein*) and the Concert House (*Konzerthaus*), and we hardly give a thought to what is meant by these casual abbreviations.

The *Gesellschaft der Musikfreunde* in Vienna was founded in 1812. It has been housed in its own building since the end of the last century, and has, in the opinion of all music lovers and strangely enough even that of the experts on acoustics, the most beautiful and best concert hall in the world. The Society was founded by a member of the imperial family and a number of aristocratic supporters. Yet it was a non-aristocratic institution at a time when the high aristocracy was only beginning to give up its obligations to act as the sponsors of the arts.

The Society acted, from the beginning, not so much as a sponsor of concerts, but as a teaching institution. The Conservatory, later called the Music Academy, and now, at long last, the Academy of Music and Representative Arts, was created by the non-aristocratic Association of Music Lovers. All the great music interpreters associated with Vienna have had a close affiliation with this Society.

In its early days it also offered some concerts as can be ascertained from the Society's reports. Franz Schubert, for instance, who was a member of the board of directors of the Society, has been called modest, because virtually none of his own compositions appeared on the programs. Most of the leading musicians—and I here speak of musicians in a double sense: active and creative, i.e. playing and composing, which were not clearly distinguished at the time—were either members or gladly allowed themselves to be nominated as honorary members.

With the move of the institution from its original, very confined quarters to the splendid new building on the Karlsplatz, the bourgeois period of Viennese music really began. The great musicians were either on the board of directors or merely sought to have some of their works on the Society's programs. The most important interpreters played in their concerts. The wealthiest Viennese devoted their time and money to its affairs. The archives of the Society were enriched by substantial gifts or bequests, so that today it is no doubt the best-endowed and most exciting private music collection in the world. The Conservatory flourished under the most esteemed teachers, and because the students always worked side by side with the most important musicians in Vienna, they were able to gain practical experience by first-hand observation. The Society as a whole profited by having its own choir which was at one time conducted by Johannes Brahms and later by other leading choral musicians.

As for the actual building, it became the center of musical life in part by virtue of its lessees: the piano manufacturer Bösendorfer has his offices there as does the Vienna Philharmonic and the music publishers Universal Edition whose reputation is international. Their stock of music fills the basement.

The way of arranging concerts has gradually changed in the 20th century. Whereas various associations or concert agents willing to assume the risk promoted guest concerts or subscription series in earlier years, the Society itself had to play the role of promoter

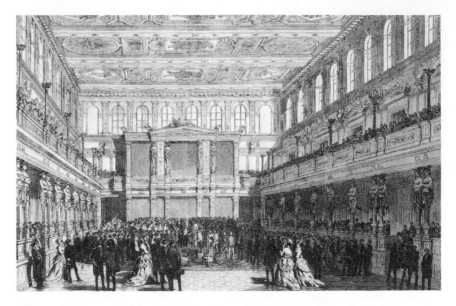

The world-famous "golden hall" of the Vienna Friends of Music on the Karlsplatz at its inauguration in the presence of Emperor Francis Joseph I on January 5, 1870. Today the candelabra on the gallery are missing and the caryatides in front of the boxes have been discreetly removed to the back of the sidewalls. But there is still no doubt about the superb acoustics of the hall.

during the inter-war years and, even more so, after World War II. Today private music promotional initiatives have almost disappeared in Vienna, above all for the understandable reason that no promoter likes to go bankrupt, whereas the Society has some security in guaranteed financial aid. In short the Society is one of the great promoters of concerts today—in contrast to the Concert Hall Association (Konzerthausgesellschaft)—although a very conservative one. The Society's programs heed the more sedate tastes of the public, not plagued by the temptation to experiment.

The former Conservatory is no longer housed in the building, yet there are always complaints that there is a shortage of space. Every opportunity to rent the large hall with its world-famous acoustics is snapped up by ensembles, by record or film producing companies, to make music before the microphones and cameras.

There is no doubt: the *Musikverein,* as it is generally and briefly referred to in Vienna, was once an association of Viennese music enthusiasts. Today it is, above all, the "Golden Concert Hall," well known to all the world thanks to the many, many telecasts and broadcasts, and the reports of enthusiastic musicians and friends of music.

The Vienna Concert Hall Society
(Konzerthausgesellschaft)

Just before World War I a second generation of wealthy Viennese citizens gathered who were of the opinion that the building of the Society of Friends of Music on the Karlsplatz was no longer sufficient to satisfy the needs of the Viennese. They wanted to erect a second concert hall and, at the same time, a multi-purpose building in which not only concerts, but functions of a social nature could take place. They thought of grand dances, of congresses, of festivals of all kinds, and even of moving the Academy of Music or Conservatory, as it was still called, from its cramped space in the *Musikverein*, preferably to a building of its own.

The opening of the building which had not yet been finished in all its parts was celebrated in 1913. The Emperor came, Richard Strauss composed a fanfare, and a large and high-ranking committee looked after its affairs.

Quite different from today's situation, neither the Concert Hall Society nor the Society of Friends of Music were promoters of concerts. Private promoters engaged guests from abroad and local orchestras which played at the promoters' financial risk or at the risk of the performers. The Society directors were nothing more than booking agents for the concert halls which they also rented to public speakers like Karl Kraus or his antagonists, or to Adolf Loos, to dance promoters, etc.

World War I dashed the plan for making the *Konzerthaus* a center of social life: There were no more large balls, no more money for glittering social occasions. And after the war one was satisfied to simply preserve what had been created. It was out of the question to finish, for instance, the intended restaurant facilities with their large kitchens.

After World War II a strange situation developed that basically set the character of Vienna's concert life thereafter: At the Music Society's hall the important international soloists and ensembles again performed their customary conservative, popular programs, while at the *Konzerthaus*, on the other hand, interested Viennese audiences discovered all the music that the Nazi government had banned as being "decadent" or by composers of the enemy. They offered an unheard-of repertoire. Composers that since then have become classics of this century were presented at long last: Béla Bartók, Paul Hindemith, the late works of Richard Strauss, as well as the young French and English, and a few Austrians whose works had not been allowed.

At the same time it became clear that there would never again be enough concert promoters and that the main burden of presenting attractive programs and taking the associated financial risks would remain that of the two principal concert societies: The *Musikverein* carried on a rich legacy of music while the *Konzerthaus* became famous for innovation.

Nothing has basically changed in that respect. Most encounters with modern music take place at the *Konzerthaus* which, however, also offers programs of traditional music in their subscription concerts. All guest artists and orchestras are somehow divided among both Societies, in a way that is difficult to fathom, so it would be unfair to give preference to one or the other institution.

The *Konzerthaus* had a complete overhaul in recent years, and now has an "Art-

Deco" or "Art Nouveau" look which is quite fashionable. It can never come up to the popularity of the *Musikverein,* but it is at least as important as the latter.

The Academy of Music and Performing Arts

That a City of Music needs the means to ensure musical education seems obvious—how could it be otherwise? Today a dense network of music schools scattered all over the city trains even the youngest Viennese musicians. For those who want to continue profession-ally, there is the appropriate Academy that can look back on a proud history. 1817 is con-sidered the date of its foundation, because in that year the Court Kapellmeister, Antonio Salieri, personally undertook the training of boys and girls in choral singing, thus putting his experience as a pedagogue at the disposal of the school that soon was to become the Conservatory. This school, at which the city's leading instrumentalists acted as instructors and correspondingly brilliant students were enrolled, existed right into the 20th century. Needless to say teachers of composition and music theory were employed as well as instructors for the instrumental classes. Composers who studied there carried names like Gustav Mahler or Hugo Wolf, and the instrumentalists became the nucleus of the Court Opera and the Philharmonic or, in some cases, famous soloists. Yet, for the sake of fair-ness, let us be modest and admit that the number of really great virtuosos who came through the Vienna schools was always small.

There are stories relating to the Academy: among them the one that Eusebius Mandyczewski, Johannes Brahms' constant assistant, taught at the Conservatory but gave more serious and successful instruction privately. And another tells of the composers around Schönberg who would not dream of setting foot in the Academy, for indeed the institution, even when Franz Schmidt took over its direction, was a conservative school for good, solid musicians. It was only after World War II that it became really "open-minded" when, under the tutelage of somewhat conservative musicians like Karl Schiske and Alfred Uhl, a generation of avant-garde musicians grew up benevolently encouraged by their teachers who did not put a straight-jacket on them.

As far as instrumental lessons were concerned, a kind of positive inbreeding seems to have been the hallmark of the Academy. The professors are the leading Viennese musi-cians who, aside from their participation as active members of orchestras or quartets, are anxious to train a young generation of musicians. Other cities are of the opinion that tradi-tion must be instituted or invented; Vienna has always led the field. The traditional Viennese school of violin playing, for example, is handed down by members of the Phil-harmonic to the younger generation of future members of the orchestra. And so it is with the other instruments: a tradition is carefully nourished, so that their players will also find places in the Vienna ensembles.

The Max Reinhardt Seminar, which is part of the Academy, has next to no influence on the training of young opera singers. Its students are put on the stage in as untrained a condition as elsewhere, so it is difficult to say whether there are more of them in Vienna than elsewhere.

The "image" of the Academy has made its imprint above all on students from abroad. They come from all the corners of the globe to study in Vienna, for at least a few semesters, in order to experience something that is still recognized as the Viennese style. That is to say that the Academy benefits from the reputation of the City of Music that is Vienna, which in turn could hardly retain its high repute without its Academy.

Musical Walks

Let us assume then that the interested reader comes from abroad and has only a short stay in the city, yet wishes to get to know it better as the City of Music by visiting some of the sites, rather than simply by reading the preceding chapters. At least two opportunities offer themselves. First of all, he could construct a list of addresses of the many places where these often restless musicians of repute have lived or worked. The list would amaze by its length—almost like a street index of Vienna—showing where there is or should be a plaque saying: In this place lived or worked this or that musician. . . . Secondly, he could select a few of these places and concentrate on a few famous composers, leaving out buildings that, in the course of time, have greatly changed from their original condition. Such an approach would still result in quite an impressive list, leaving it to the reader to choose from it.

I will try to do it differently: I shall introduce a few "addresses" that can be visited within the span of 2–3 days without any exertion, and which, in my opinion, would give a good idea of what today's Vienna can offer of the near or distant past: Some idea of the "flair" of the City of Music.

The reader starts with a visit to the building on the Karlsplatz that houses the Society of Friends of Music. Even during the day it is an amazing treasure trove of music and, no doubt, someone can be persuaded (with or without a tip or a few kind words) to allow one a glimpse of the famous "Golden Hall." Once that far, do not miss a glance at the "Brahmssaal," the chamber music hall of the building. Perhaps you might, at first sight, not deem them as beautiful as some Viennese music lovers do. But both have such a concentration of music history packed into them that it can be felt even in the light of day. In the Great Hall note the Director's box in which Brahms sat. One simply has to imagine what it means when in the standing room at the rear, under the balcony, the musical youth of today listens to a concert. Hugo Wolf stood there once and was annoyed by the Viennese who laughed at Bruckner. In the Brahms Hall many of the concerts of the Schönberg Society took place, and it remains the most typical Viennese chamber music hall. The acoustics in both spaces are, according to the unanimous opinion of the experts, unequalled in all the world.

Next I would advise any visitor to have the Court Chapel opened to him, even if it requires persistence with the keeper in charge. In the nearly undecorated church not only many weddings, but also many funeral services for members of the Habsburg family took place. Franz Schubert sang there. Anton Bruckner played the organ and almost every Viennese musician gave of his best playing there. After leaving the Court Chapel walk the few minutes to the Michaelerplatz (St. Michael's Square) and look at the building at the corner of the Kohlmarkt next to the church. Haydn lived in the attic there, froze, made music and waited for a secure position. Some of the houses in the neighborhood are, of course, of later construction, but the basic appearance is still reminiscent of the time of Haydn. The visitor standing on the Michaelerplatz has to imagine that the "Theater at the Kärntner Tor" used to stand less than a stone's throw from there, so that Haydn almost literally was able to see from his window the throng of people going to the theater. No doubt, it was very noisy and exciting in the Inner City, especially around the *Hofburg* or Imperial Castle.

Next, a walk of about half a minute to the Josefsplatz (Joseph's Square) is recommended. There once stood the big wooden structure of the theater that Lodovico Burnacini built, in which the Emperor's operas were performed. Nearby is the unobtrusive entrance to the Redoutensäle (Court Ballrooms) where, one after another, the members of the Strauss dynasty played for the court balls and where countless concerts were given.

Now walk another ten minutes past the State Opera, to the Naschmarkt (Produce Market), so reminiscent of old times, site of the "Theater an der Wien" (Theater on the Vienna River). The theater is barely visible from the front, because its frontage has been integrated into the facade of a block of apartments. But at the side the old Papageno Gate still stands, offering a pleasant view of the old theater building, still intact. Do not forget that, although *The Magic Flute* was not premiered here, Beethoven's *Fidelio* in all its versions was, and later many of the best known operettas opened here. A visit for a performance gives the impression of an old-fashioned theater, even though the many renovations since 1900 have altered the original condition.

If tired, you might go back into the Inner City near St. Stephen's Cathedral where, in the Grünangergasse at the inn "Zum Grünen Anker" (To the Green Anchor), you can refresh yourself. This is a place which has changed very little since the time of Schubert and which was and still is a frequent meeting place of many Viennese musicians and artists. I can state, without any qualms of conscience, that it preserves the real atmosphere which composers enjoyed without trying to attract tourist business.

Most of the coffee houses along the Ringstrasse where, around the turn of the century, "serious" composers as well as the heroes of the operetta were assembled, have now disappeared or have been renovated so that their former character has disappeared. However, the "Green Anchor" has been in the possession of the same family for many generations and has not undergone any modernization. It is a good example of the restaurants that played their part in the lives of the great masters, and it has survived them.

If you have time to visit only one of Beethoven's many abodes, take a cab to the Eroica House, where he wrote his "Heiligenstädter Testament" (Heiligenstadt Last Will and Testament). It has been lovingly restored and much of the rural charm of his time has been preserved. Here you can imagine more clearly than at other Beethoven residences that Heiligenstadt was at that time far outside the city and that a musician could go for long walks in the still rural neighborhood and almost forget imperial Vienna. A second Beethoven house at the Pfarrplatz (Vicarage Square) can easily be visited on the same occasion. There are also a number of well-known "Heuriger" (wine taverns) in the area, but these Heuriger no longer possess the "atmosphere" they must have had at the time of Beethoven. I would advise you to visit a single establishment, rather than taking a tour.

On your way back to town you may want to acquaint yourself with scenes of Schubert's childhood: His birthplace in the Nussdorfer Strasse has been carefully restored to its original condition; only the small recital hall on the ground floor postdates Schubert's time. The visitor need add but one element in his imagination: He must realize that the house was, at that time, a large rental property in which the entire Schubert family lived in very confined quarters.

If you are interested in Johannes Brahms, the Archives of the Friends of Music Society mentioned earlier are, beyond doubt, the richest source of information, for they were bequeathed the composer's manuscripts and his entire library. You can see the books Brahms preferred, and can marvel at the number of marginal notes he made. Don't let the term "archives" scare or discourage you: you can be assured of a friendly and helpful attitude from all who look after your needs. In general, you need not be put off by a closed door or by the posted official times of opening. Wherever you really want to see something, you have to try—as in Italy—to get in, irrespective of "officialdom."

The other possible Brahms sites are not that exciting. The house where he lived has been demolished, but one memorial room is intact: If you set out to find Joseph Haydn's traces in Vienna you may see one room in the Haydn house that has been dedicated to Brahms' memory, put there for reasons of economy.

So this then is the Haydn house! It has been preserved throughout the centuries, because the Viennese loved and respected him, both while he was alive and after his death. At Haydngasse 19 in the Sixth District, everything is more or less as it was, and you literally are in the rooms that the aging master, then world famous, inhabited in his last years, still working and composing the two great oratorios, some Masses, and what became the Austrian National Anthem. It was in these rooms that he received visitors from all over Europe, and it was here that he died as Napoleon entered the city ordering that a guard of honor be posted in front of the building. Even today you can feel something of the quiet genius who was only slightly overshadowed by Mozart and Beethoven, but remains a shining light.

Not far from there (IVth District, Mühlgasse 28) one should look at the Ehrbar concert hall—not too strenuous an undertaking. This is a small recital hall erected by the piano manufacturer of that name which was not—unlike the famed Bösendorfer Hall—demolished, and is still in use. Numerous celebrities were guests in this hall, and here Brahms played some of his own works as well as Schubert's compositions, for he (Brahms) was an accomplished pianist, a fact that even Brahms experts tend to forget. He managed to draw audiences as an outstanding if not virtuoso pianist. Moreover, this hall gives an idea of how concerts of importance were given in by-gone days, not only in the two great concert halls, but also elsewhere, and how small and modest these places often were.

These then are the key places to see on a short visit to Vienna. But we must acknowledge that living music cannot be captured in these places, but lives on in opera performances and concerts only at the places where they are now presented.

Those having an interest in visiting the graves of any of these masters may go to the Zentralfriedhof (Central Cemetery) where their memorial graves are located. Their remains, however, were transferred to this place only at the end of the last century. One can also go to the Grinzing cemetery to look at the modest, but artistically most satisfying grave stone of Gustav Mahler, designed by Josef Hoffmann. Now that the world has come to a better opinion of Mahler, we have become accustomed to pilgrimages to his grave, for, after all, he himself returned to Vienna just before he died, only to be buried here.

I also urge a walk through Vienna's Stadtpark (City Park) as worthwhile, not only because it is a most attractive park, set out at the time of the construction of the great Ringstrasse and its buildings, but also because it was frequented by a number of Viennese musicians. In summer, the strains of a large orchestra that plays before the *Kursalon* can be heard, thus adding to the atmosphere, and as inspiringly as at the time of Johann Strauss. Again some readers might reproach me for promoting a privately owned establishment. But I would reply that the visitor to the Music City of Vienna need not be bothered about who manages to recreate the music that has always sounded here.

Index of Persons

Sources of Illustrations

P. 10: Vienna Choir Boys.

P. 12, 13, 99: Wilhelm Beetz, *Das Wiener Opernhaus 1869–1945*. Zürich, 1949.

P. 15 (below), 31, 93, 94, 96: Austrian National Library.

P. 20, 64–65: Franz Endler.

P. 15 (above), 18–19, 25, 27, 46–47, 49, 51, 60–61, 74, 89, 92: Historical Museum of the City of Vienna.

P. 22: Bibliothèque-Musée de l'Opéra de Paris.

P. 24: Georg N. von Nissen, *Biographie von W. A. Mozart.* Leipzig, 1828.

P. 26: E. Schikaneder, *Die Zauberflöte,* facsimile of the first edition of 1791. Vienna, 1924.

P. 29: *Beethoven.* Vienna, Munich, Basel, 1963.

P. 35, 37, 38: Otto Erich Deutsch, *Franz Schubert.* Munich, Leipzig, 1913.

P. 45, 79: Rudolf Wolkan, *Wiener Volkslieder aus fünf Jahrhunderten.* Vienna, 1926.

P. 54–55: Dr. Andreas von Beckerath.

P. 57, 110: Archiv der Gesellschaft der Musikfreunde, Vienna.

P. 68, 71: *Schönberg-Webern-Berg* Exhibition catalog. Vienna, 1969.

P. 83, 85: Otto Schneidereit, *Franz Lehár.* Berlin, 1984.

P. 88: Luzi Korngold, *erich wolfgang korngold* [sic]. Vienna, 1967.

P. 95: Alexander Witeschnik, *Wiener Opernkunst.* Vienna, 1959.